Duncan Edwards The Full Report
A Britespot Publication

First Published in Great Britain by
Britespot Publishing Solutions Limited
Chester Road, Cradley Heath, West Midlands B64 6AB

July 2001

ISBN 0 9539 2885 3

Printed and bound in Great Britain by
Cradley Print Limited, Chester Road, Cradley Heath, West Midlands B64 6AB

Cover design and layout © Legends In Print Limited

The Author Iain McCartney

Born and bred north of Hadrians Wall, but a lifelong Manchester United supporter and has been travelling south to watch them since the late sixties. He has contributed to many other books and magazines and currently contributes to two United supporters club magazines and as a keen collector of United memorabilia has run the United Collectors Club for the past 11 years.

He says that United is in his blood as a distant relation - John McCartney captained Newton Heath in the early 1890's.

Acknowledgments

I would like to thank Britespot Publishing Solutions Limited in agreeing to publish and help make this book a unique insight into the tragically short but phenomenal career of Duncan Edwards.

I would also like to thank Mrs Sarah-Anne Edwards for all her help and support in the compilation of this book with photos and invaluable information about her son. In addition, I would also like to acknowledge the considerable help received from Football Heroes in Stourbridge, West Midlands, not only with photographs and memorabilia but for allowing the original print of Duncan Edwards to be used on the cover of this book.

The comments and anecdotes from former colleagues who played with and against Duncan at Manchester United and England, including Ray Barlow, Ronnie Clayton, Jack Crompton, David Gaskell, Wilf McGuiness, Kenny Morgan, Albert Scanion, Nigel Simms, Jeff Whitefoot, Graham Williams, Ray Wood and Bobby Robson, were also a great source of inspiration.

Finally, my thanks to Dudley Metropolitan Borough Council and Manchester United Museum and Tour Centre for allowing archive material relating to Duncan Edwards to be photographed and reproduced in this publication.

DUNCAN EDWARDS
THE FULL REPORT
By Iain McCartney

CONTENTS

UNITED REVIEW

MANCHESTER
UNITED
FOOTBALL CLUB

UNITED
v
CARDIFF CITY

Kick-off 3-0 p.m.

4th APRIL

4d

NUMBER 19

1952-53
SEASON PROGRAMME

OFFICIAL

MANCHESTER UNITED F.C.

Photo by courtesy of the Pro——

Back Row (left to right): Downie, Rowley, Aston, Allen, Ch——
Front Row (left to right): Berry, Carey, Cockburn, and ——
F.A. Charity Shield (left), and the First Division Champion——

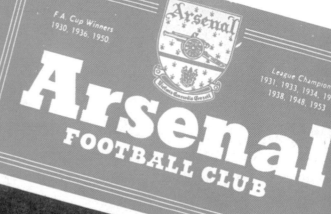

Arsenal
FOOTBALL CLUB

F.A. Cup Winners
1930, 1936, 1950.

League Champions
1931, 1933, 1934, 1935,
1938, 1948, 1953

Season 1957-8

Football League Division I

ARSENAL v. MANCHESTER UNITED

Saturday, 1st February

KICK-OFF 3 p.m. (Part Floodlight)

OFFICIAL

6d

PROGRAMME

FOREWORD

The message below was sent by Martin Edwards, Chairman of Manchester United for the Duncan Edwards Tribute Dinner which took place on Thursday 15th March 2001. The Dinner saw friends and colleagues of Duncan Edwards meet together to pay tribute to a unique football phenomenon.

A MESSAGE FROM MANCHESTER UTD

"Duncan Edwards was, quite simply, one of the finest footballers ever to wear the red shirt of Manchester United. Among the many wonderful players to emerge from Matt Busby's inspired youth policy during the early 1950s, Duncan was the most outstanding. His talent was extraordinary, and his contribution to the team during his tragically short career helped the team to win two English league championships and become a potent force in European football. I remember as a very young boy watching him play, and I know from my many years at United that his reputation as a player among his contemporaries was second to none. Sir Bobby Charlton has told me on many occasions that Duncan was the finest footballer he ever played with or against, a category that includes such legends as Pele and George Best. There can be no finer tribute than that. At Manchester United, Duncan Edwards will never be forgotten."

MARTIN EDWARDS
CHAIRMAN

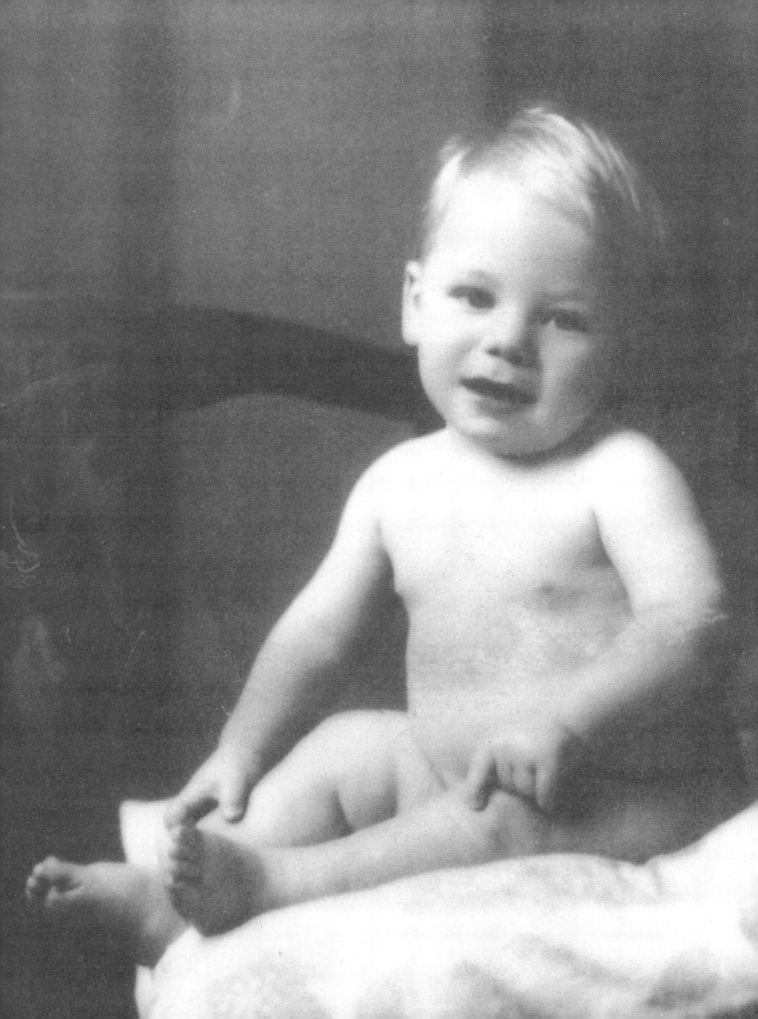

CHAPTER ONE
SCUFFED SHOES AND DIRTY KNEES

It wasn't that the scratched ink stained and rusted desk was too small for the fidgeting, tousle haired primary schoolboy, it was after all, the one that he had sat behind for some time. Neither was it unusual for the youngster to show signs of impatience around this time of the afternoon, as the minute hand on the clock at the back of the classroom ticked closer to the end of another school day. His mind was now far away from multiplication, the capitals of the world or memorable dates in history and firmly fixed on yet another after school kick about with his friends.

For Duncan Edwards, like hundreds of other boys of his generation and many more before and after, football was the be all and end all of his young life. There was no television, computer games or whatever else the modern day schoolboy wastes away the hours with, as the boys (and girls) in those poverty stricken, disrupted days immediately after the Second World War had to make their own entertainment, and his release from the rigors of school work and life at home was football.

He was born on October 1st 1936 at 23 Malvern Crescent, Holly Hall, Dudley in the heart of the Black Country, a reference to the area's industrial heritage. But along with his father Gladstone and mother Sarah, he was soon to move to 31 Elm Road, in the town's Priory Estate, where Duncan was to spend most of his young life.

Three decades ago, child birth could have its problems and the early days and years of a child's life could see them suffer from all sorts of disease and illnesses. The Edwards' family, like countless others, finding this out to their cost as ten years later when Duncan's sister, Carol Anne died at the age of fourteen weeks. However, Sarah Edwards had no worries or problems regarding the health of her son who weighed in at nine and a half pounds and continued to progress as the weeks and months passed by.

From an early age, the sturdy youngster showed an interest in anything that could be kicked with his parents having to make allowances for his somewhat obsessive craving for a ball. Everywhere he went, a ball was never far away. When his parents went visiting and the last minute warning of "don't you dare bring that ball with you" and been administered, it was more often than not smuggled out of the house in a coat pocket or wherever and when the conversations were in full swing at their destination, Duncan would slip outside and the ball was produced. When he was discovered, his parents could only shake their head and they eventually gave up trying to separate him from his beloved ball.

His parents could not be too critical of his interest in the game, as both sides of the family had footballing connections. His father played at amateur level, partnering his brother George at full back for a local side in the Cradley Heath League, while his mother's father had also played the game at this level. His uncle, Ray Westwood, played as a professional with Bolton Wanderers in the 1930's and also represented England. Much to their relief, however, Duncan did enjoy other boyish activities such as cricket and fishing, as well as being a member of the local Boy Scout troop.

The pre school days passed quickly and the bell at Priory Road Junior School was soon summoning young master Edwards beyond the gates he had often passed with his parents. The school was only a few hundred yards from the Edwards' home and neighbours were soon accustomed to the familiar sight of the schoolboy in short trousers dribbling his tennis ball past lamp posts and imaginary opponents on his way to and from lessons.

"He didn't mind going to school", his mother was to recall in later years, "and he enjoyed drawing and history, but he always preferred to be out of doors".

When he was considered big enough, rather than old enough, he was selected for the Priory Road school team, a collection of individuals who won some and lost some, making little impression in the local school league or in cup competitions. However, with the addition of Duncan Edwards to the ranks, there was a vast improvement in performances and success was soon to be achieved in local competitions.

Mr Gordon Meddings, who was later to teach at Priory Road, remembered his first sighting of the talented schoolboy in an inter school match, when his St John's side were in opposition. "Duncan was only ten years old at the time" he recalled, " but even then it was clearly noticeable that he possessed a talent for the game. I cannot remember what position he was meant to be playing, but he covered every inch of the park and was involved in everything from the taking of goal kicks to throw ins and corners. He was also on hand to thwart any attacks made by my lads, playing a big part in his team winning 3-0."

"...I wrote to a friend and told him I had seen a boy of eleven who would play for England one day"

The eleven year old schoolboy was also remembered by Mr Geoffrey Groves who also recalled seeing him in a primary school fixture. "He'd got back from hop picking that morning and gone straight into the school team, dominating the whole match. He told the other twenty one players what to do, and the referee and linesmen as well. When I got home, I wrote to a friend and told him I had seen a boy of eleven who would play for England one day"

Duncan and his school team mates put in hours of practise, especially during the summer days when they could be found at Netherton Park or Priory Park, or to be honest on any patch of waste ground where a kick about was taking place. It was if he could hear the thud of shoe or boot against a ball from any distance or even smell a kick about taking place, he was always involved. Geoffrey Groves often watched those disorganised kick abouts and in an assessment of Duncan in later years commented, "the young Edwards was never afraid to go in and tackle. He had legs and thighs already like oak trees, and yet was so amazingly light on his feet. He could almost have played blindfolded. Admittedly, he had a 'big mouth', coming from a rough tough background, but I do not think anyone ever took exception as his advice like his play was so impressive. He quietened down considerably by the time he reached fourteen.

In the autumn of 1948, shortly before his twelfth birthday, Duncan moved to Wolverhampton Street Secondary School. Many of his footballing friends continued their education at the Park Secondary School, but it has been suggested that Duncan decided to attend Wolverhampton Street School as he wanted to join their very successful Morris and Sword dancing team! Whether that is correct I have no idea, but shortly after joining the school, he did indeed transfer his nibble footwork from the muddy playing fields to the school hall and became a member of the senior dance team, such was his talent for this recreational activity. A notable inclusion for a first year pupil.

Football was obviously still his first love and he immediately stepped into the Wolverhampton Street junior side, filling the centre half position, mainly due to his physique and also taking on the role of captain. Because of his size, quite often head and shoulders above team mates and opponents alike, he stood out during the games, but his performances and potential also made him conspicuous to all those who frequented the touch line at those fixtures. Members of the Dudley Schools selection committee were amongst those who took note of his performances and they soon considered him worthy of a place in their side even although he was only twelve, while most of the other team members and indeed the opposition were fifteen.

The lad from the Priory Estate's must have been considered something of an exceptional individual as he was selected to play for the Dudley Schools' side, not in his normal school position of centre half, but in the somewhat alien outside left berth. It was felt that the central defensive role was too physical a position even for Duncan to fill at this level and indeed any middle of the park position might find the newcomer caught up in some unnecessary and untoward involvement, so, because they wanted him in the team the selectors felt that at outside left he was away from the more involved areas of play.

Secretary of the Dudley Schools Football Association at that time was Mr Eric Booth, who explained that "although a well built lad for his age he was about to come face to face with older and bigger opposition for possibly the first time at competitive level and in order to keep him protected and in case he was overawed, it was decided to play him on the wing".

Alongside Duncan, at inside left, in that Dudley Schools side was his second cousin, Dennis Stevens who captained the side and although there was some three years of an age difference and Dennis attended a different school, his younger cousin's football reputation went before him.

During Duncan's second year at Wolverhampton Street his footballing diary became near to overflowing with selection not just for his school side, but also Dudley Boys, Worcester County XI, Birmingham and District XI and the England Schools under 14 team. He cared little for whom or where he played or indeed what position. If there was a game and he was chosen to take part in it then he was happy.

The free for all, multi-sided games were also still regularly played and in later years Duncan was to write about one such 'fixture'. "Every evening and Sunday morning I would be in the park with lads of nineteen or twenty," he wrote, "getting used to the hurly burly of the game, and giving , I hoped, as good as I took. For most of these games I would play in my ordinary walking shoes, a fact that caused friction at home. On one occasion my mother bought me a new pair of shoes and within a couple of hours of putting them on I arrived home with them invisible beneath great cakes of mud. My popularity was at a low ebb that night".

Duncan's parents were completely unaware that their son was playing with grown men. It was actually only by chance that his mother found out, as one day she was passing a park and turned upon hearing a cry "go on Duncan". There was her son giving it everything amid what were obviously a much older collection of players. A couple of the older boys, who recognised Mrs Edwards, abandoned there involvement in the game and went over to reassure her that she had no need to worry and that her son was more than capable of looking after himself.

Gordon Meddings, who had encountered the young titan at junior school became more closely involved with Duncan as he progressed through the county sides to England level. "Although well built and not adverse to using this to his advantage, Duncan always played the game fairly," emphasised Gordon. "However, on one occasion he was involved in a tackle with an opponent during a Birmingham and District trial match, which resulted in the other youngster breaking his leg.
"No blame was attached to Duncan whatsoever, it was just one of those unfortunate things, but the following week when Duncan took the field for a Dudley Schools match in Birmingham the youngster, with his leg in plaster, was standing on the touch line. This had a very noticeable effect on Duncan and for once, his performance was well below par and I think the incident remained in the back of his mind for some time".

One other match that was recalled by Gordon Meddings was in the Worcester County Trophy at the Dudley Sports Centre, the home of Dudley Town Football Club, against Evesham. This particular match was played in rather adverse conditions with a very strong wind blowing down the pitch, which resulted in the ball going everywhere except into the back of the net. At half time it was suggested to Duncan that the only way to score was for him to have a go by himself.
As the second half progressed, Duncan gathered the ball in his own penalty area and set off towards the opposition goal. Amazingly, he dribbled his way down the field and with the goalkeeper at his mercy fired in a shot which cannoned off the 'keepers legs and rebounded the length of the pitch, going out for a goal kick at the opposite end.

Like Gordon Meddings, Eric Booth took a close interest in the development of this multi-talented youngster and recommended Duncan for a place in the England under 14 international trial at Oldham, never really expecting him to be selected as he was after all only twelve. Surprisingly, the England Schools Association decided the Dudley youngster was worth his place in the side and what was even more surprising was the fact that he has selected to play in the centre forward position. Centre half, left half, outside left and now centre forward. Where next?

His appearance in the international trial was almost a non-starter and brought disappointment to many of his fellow schoolmates and teachers. On the same day as the trial, he was due to take part in the National Morris and Sword Dancing Festival at Derby and having already competed in the Birmingham and Leamington festivals it was hoped that his presence would inspire the school to success at Derby. There was little chance that the Festival would take precedence over the England trial and while the dancers went south to Derby, Duncan journeyed north to Oldham.

At the end of an eventful afternoon, the twelve year old was certainly convinced that he had made the correct choice when his name was read out as a member of the England side to face Ireland on May 6th with Oldham's Boundary Park again the venue.

The six page programme covering this fixture, which England won 5-2, is certainly nothing special but for Duncan Edwards it not only marked his debut in the white shirt of England, but the first real step on the ladder of success. Turning to the team page, few of the names mean anything today, certainly none of the Irish side stir the memory. But, for the record, the England team read as follows....A.J.Silver (Maidenhead), J.Woodward (Islington) J.F.Middlemass (E.Northumberland), P.R.Marton (York), M.Underwood (Kettering), W.P.Oldham (Ellesmere Port), H.Collier (Horwich), A.Farrell (Wirral), D.Edwards (Dudley), R.Parry – captain (Derby) and D.Pegg (Doncaster).

Turning to the page containing the player pen pictures, it carried a rather prophetic heading – "These Boys Are The Stars Of Today – Keep An Eye On Them, They Will Be The Stars Of Tomorrow". The pen picture of each boy was no more than a couple of lines and alongside D. Edwards (Dudley) was written – 'Worcester County player. Strong and two footed. Splendid distributor, especially with long cross passes to wing'. Remember, this was written about a twelve year old schoolboy!

It is worth picking up on the mention of Duncan being 'two footed' as this was part of the game that he had spent many hours perfecting and was later to discuss at length. He wrote, "my own weakness was the left foot. Constantly I tried to transfer the ball to my right, so losing time and opportunities. Mr Booth concentrated on making me left foot conscious. His main task was to talk confidence into me.

"For an hour at a stretch I would bang a ball against a rough brick wall and meet the rebound with whichever foot was suitable. Then I would try bouncing the ball from one instep to the other, so that the left began to get the feel of the ball as naturally as did the right.

"My reward now is a left foot that I can rely upon. In shooting, it packs as much power as my right..."

"The natural testing ground for my left foot was the park in the evening games among the local lads. There it was of little importance if I made an error. I could slice a left foot clearance far behind my own goal without feeling as if the end of the earth had come. I started using my left when I was in the clear with the ball and unharried by the other side. As it strengthened, so I began to use it when I was in difficulties, and eventually I would try to go through the whole of these games (and remember that they would go on from tea until it was too dark to see the ball) using my left foot.

"My reward now is a left foot that I can rely upon. In shooting, it packs as much power as my right, even if the direction is not quite so finely controlled".

The Wolverhampton Street School team came under the guidance of the aforementioned Gordon Meddings, who not surprisingly took more than a passing interest in Duncan's footballing career. Mr Meddings was enthusiastic in his coaching and like any aspiring player always set his sights to a higher level, with the aim of achieving an FA Coaching Award he was one of the many teachers who went on an FA Coaching course held at Blackpool in August 1950.

The 'class' for such courses was made up from members of the current England under 14 and under 15 sides, and Duncan was more than happy to go along with Gordon Meddings for something of a Summer break away from the smoky, industrial environment of the West Midlands. More importantly, it meant more football.

The budding coaches and footballers were housed in a hotel on the Lancashire resorts South Shore, which was actually owned by England and Blackpool winger Stanley Matthews, who himself had played in the England schools side of 1929. Little did the starry eyed Dudley youngster know then, that he would come into closer contact with the England legend in a few years time.

It wasn't all football during the FA Coaching class at Blackpool and like today, the many attractions of the holiday resort were plentiful and tempting to the youngsters from different parts of the country, most of whom were paying their first visit to the seaside town.

Obviously, the Pleasure Beach was the main focus of their attention being close to their hotel, but it was not, however, the breathtaking Big Dipper and the other exciting rides that brought gasps of delight from the boys upon their first visit, but the discovery amongst the grander attractions of a "Beat The Goalkeeper" side show. Naturally, they all wanted to try their luck at putting the ball past the unfortunate goalkeeper and before long the unassuming stall holder was running out of prizes.

After a couple of visits, the secret was out and the owner was reluctant to let the boys exploit their talents against his naïve employee. Being a businessman, however, and realising a good thing when it was placed in front of him, he decided to offer the boys free shots in order to attract further custom to his stall.

One of the coaches at the Blackpool course was the Everton, Arsenal and England star Joe Mercer and although there to help the teachers, he took an interest in the youngsters, passing on tips and suggestions in the effort to improve their game. While in conversation with Gordon Meddings, Joe Mercer spoke at length about Duncan, singling him out for special praise as well as predicting a big future for him at professional level.

As Duncan progressed at school in the classroom, he did likewise on the football front. During his second year at Wolverhampton Street School he was once again mentioned by Eric Booth as a possible for the England Schoolboy's side and this was supported by Mr Bert Tunnicliffe who was the local English Schools FA representative, following a closer look at Duncan in competitive action.

Selection for the England under 15 side followed, (the first Dudley youngster to reach this level), with his debut against Wales at Wembley on Saturday April 7th 1951, when he filled the now familiar No.6 jersey.

The match programme for this fixture shows that only four members of the team that took the field against Ireland, almost twelve months previously were still good enough for the side. They were goalkeeper Silver, inside right Farrell, the left wing partnership of Ray Parry and David Pegg and of course Duncan. His pen picture this time around read...'Captain of Worcester County S.F.A. Selected to represent Birmingham and District S.F.A. Age 14 years 6 months. Height 5ft 8 ins Weight 10st 12lbs. He was at least a year younger than any of his team mates.

Some seven months after his Wembley debut, Duncan referred to his experience in one of his English essays, under the heading "A True Wish", in which he wrote the following...

Well it all began when I was little boy of about seven years of age. I had heard my father takeing about a place by the name of Wembly Stadium. It was a wet day in april and my uncle Gorge and dad were sitting round the fire where my uncle Gorge said to my father, "I see England are playing Scottland at Wembly next saterday", "Are they", my father replied.
I thougt to myself "now's my chance to ask them where this Wembly Stadium is while there on the subject". So I turned to my uncle and asked him where this Stadium was, and he replied, "Duncan, this Stadium as you call it is the third biggest football Stadium in the world and situated in London". I told my uncle I wish I could go there and he said I would before long. I was thirteen and I still wanted to go to Wembly and on 7th of april I was picked to play for england against wales (at Wembly Stadium). My uncle was right when he said I would some day go to Webly Stadium.

The above, by the way, is how it appeared in Duncan's English jotter.

The following season, 1951-52, brought further international recognition, with under 15 schoolboy caps, this time as captain, against Scotland twice, Wales and Eire. The Wales fixture being played almost on home ground for Duncan – St Andrews, Birmingham.

This was Duncan's penultimate appearance as a schoolboy in the white of England and once again he showed the potential of a star in the making and one of the most sought after players in the game. This included those in the professional ranks.

After the early feet finding minutes, England were first to produce any real form of attack and came close to scoring, following a move instigated by the England captain. Ward, on the England left wing, was soon on the receiving end of some excellent passes from Duncan, while another of his through balls saw Morton also come close. Against the run of play, however, Wales took the lead in the 16th minute.

"All the club's were after him as a schoolboy" ...he said that Manchester United were the greatest club in the country and nothing would stop him from going to Old Trafford"

England managed to pull level prior to the interval and as the second half progressed, Wales became increasingly pushed back onto the defensive and inevitably a second goal followed and one that was to prove the winner. By now, Duncan was the outstanding player on the pitch, starting attack after attack on the England left, exciting both the crowd and the club scouts mixed amongst them. For the latter, it was to no avail, as they had no chance of capturing his signature.

Duncan's obvious talent had long since been recognised and noted in the West Midlands, but with him now performing on a much bigger stage, a number of clubs were now being attracted to him and there was no doubt at all that he would soon be snapped up by a League club as an apprentice. It was always assumed that one of the Midland club's, such as Wolverhampton Wanderers or Aston Villa would win the race for his signature and his parents dreamed of their son signing for one of those local rivals.

"All the club's were after him as a schoolboy" said his mother, "and we would have loved him to play for the Wolves, or the Albion, or the Villa. But he said that Manchester United were the greatest club in the country and nothing would stop him from going to Old Trafford".

It is difficult to fathom out how Duncan decided that he wanted to play for Manchester United, but possibly the fact that United won the League Championship in season 1951-52, having been runners up in four of the previous five following their FA Cup success in 1948, had more than a little to do with it. His preference for Manchester United was not widely known and it was in fact another Lancashire side who made all the early running in an attempt to sign him. Bolton Wanderers had liked what they had seen and at one point even considered themselves favourite to obtain his signature.

Two of the Bolton backroom staff at that time, Frank Pickford the chief scout and George Taylor the chief coach, had watched Duncan on numerous occasions. After one particular trial match at Dudley Port, they decided to make a positive move on behalf of the club, but somehow they missed their intended target as he left the ground after the game. An enquiry as to where they might find the Edwards home was made at the local police station, directions were given and they were soon back on the scent.

Initial approaches were made to Duncan's parents and a few pints were added to the Bolton expense account in a nearby public house as the Bolton representatives attempted to tighten their grip on the young prospect through a chat with his father. Shortly afterwards, Duncan was invited up to Bolton for a look around the ground and his acceptance of the invitation helped raise their hopes of obtaining the sought after signature.

Duncan's former Dudley school's team mate and second cousin, Dennis Stevens was already at Bolton, as was his England schools captain Ray Parry, so there would have at least have been a couple of familiar faces at the club should he decide to sign. Ray Parry was even driven down to Dudley by Frank Pickford and sat in the car talking to Duncan as the Bolton scout spoke again with Gladstone and Sarah Edwards in their Elm Road home. The journey proved to be wasted, as Ray Parry was politely told "thanks for the interest, but I'm going to join Manchester United".

So, while Bolton Wanderers were doing all the running, where were Manchester United?

Obviously, there had been club representatives, in particular Reg Priest their Midlands scout, at many of the games in which Duncan was involved and his name had been noted as a potential First Division footballer. Matt Busby's backroom staff of Jimmy Murphy, Bert Whalley and Joe Armstrong had all viewed this future star and all held the same view – "sign him".

Initially, Matt Busby had set his eyes on another member of the England Schools side, inside right Alec Farrell, but during a conversation with his good friend Joe Mercer he was told that there was no way

that he was likely to secure that particular signature as the youngster, who hailed from Merseyside, was Everton mad and destined to sign for the Goodison club. Mercer, who remember had taken part in coaching sessions involving these boys, asked Busby if he was not interested in the Dudley lad, Edwards?

Busby, however, was unable to make a positive move for Duncan as he was younger than Alec Farrell and the rest of his England team mates and at that particular time, the rule book stated that a schoolboy could not sign for a professional club until the end of their international season. The Manchester United manager had to bide his time. Having a club scout, Reg Priest, practically on Duncan's doorstep helped in keeping up to date with any attempted bids from another club to secure even a verbal agreement involving the family.

Duncan's final match of his England Schoolboy season, earned him a record breaking ninth cap, and came against Eire in a friendly at Dalymount Park, Dublin on May 31st 1952. Unfortunately it was not the best of endings as for the first time at this level he tasted defeat, with the home side winning by the only goal. It was a disappointed England captain on the long journey home, but little did he know that the disappointment was going to be short lived.

The first day of June brought the travel weary schoolboy a long lie in bed, but as the day progressed it also produced a frenzy of activity in both the West Midlands and Manchester.

A telephone call from Reg Priest to Old Trafford brought the news that Bolton Wanderers were rumoured to be close to making one final attempt to persuade Duncan to sign for them. The United scout also reckoned that if the club did not make a counter move then the youngster might think that they had lost interest and that if he wanted to become a professional footballer then perhaps he should accept the Wanderers offer.

Quickly, United coach Bert Whalley was called and instructed to drive down to Dudley. He was told to speak to the Edwards' family and reassure Duncan that United did want him and arrangements would be made for him to sign. Whalley set off on his errand, but before he got anywhere near the West Midlands his car broke down, forcing him to telephone back to Old Trafford regarding his unfortunate predicament and that he was going to hitch hike home.

Upon his late night return to Manchester, he was met at Old Trafford by an anxious Jimmy Murphy who informed him that it had been decided to hire a car and that they were both going to go to Dudley that night, as a similar trip the following day could be too late. The tired Bert Whalley had no complaints as he knew how important the signing of Edwards was in the long term future of the club.

Fortunately, there were no further delays or hiccups on the return journey south, with the United pair breathing a sigh of relief as they drove into Elm Road to find the place in darkness, with no cars or representatives of other clubs' encamped outside the Edwards' house. Although it was now the early hours of the morning, there was nothing else for Murphy and Whalley to do except awaken the sleeping household. So, making as little noise as possible, in the hope that they would not awaken the whole street, Bert Whalley knocked on the door.

There were a few antagonising moments before a noise could be heard from inside the house and Gladstone Edwards' could be imagined stomping down the stairs muttering ' who the bloody hell is knocking on my door at this hour of the morning?' Slowly the door was eased open and the half awake features of Duncan's father peered round the edge.

Apologises, and an explanation were quickly made by the United duo as they were ushered into the family living room where Sarah Edwards was already seated having also been awaked by the Manchester intruders. Minutes later a pyjama clad, sleepy eyed schoolboy was standing alongside his similarly attired father and as he rubbed the sleep from his eyes he signed for Manchester United.
Somewhat unmoved by it all, Duncan was quick to ask his nocturnal visitors what all the fuss was about as he had already said to manager Matt Busby that Manchester United was the only club he wanted to join.

It was 2am on the morning of June 2nd 1952. Duncan Edwards was now a Manchester United player.

Surprisingly, there are a few conflicting stories to Duncan's early morning signing for United. One states that it was Matt Busby himself who made the moonlit journey to Dudley to make the signing, but in the late Jimmy Murphy's autobiography "Matt United and Me" (Souvenir Press 1968) there is no mention of Busby's involvement in the visit to the Edwards' household.

..."Still half dazed, I made my way into the light of the sitting room to come face to face for the first time with Matt Busby, the manager of Manchester United..."

The most surprising reference to the signing comes in Duncan's own posthumous book "Tackle Soccer This Way" (Stanley Paul 1958). Within its pages comes the following…

"Came the day of my sixteenth birthday I retired to bed after the usual round of celebrations and over eating. At two o'clock in the morning the family was awakened by a knock at the door.

"I heard my father go downstairs but I was too tired to take much notice. I turned over and tried to go to sleep again. A few minutes later my bedroom door opened and my father said: 'Slip something on and come downstairs. There's somebody to see you.'

"Still half dazed, I made my way into the light of the sitting room to come face to face for the first time with Matt Busby, the manager of Manchester United. He had known better than I about the interest other clubs had taken in me, and he wanted to be the first to talk to my parents. So he had driven through the night from Manchester.

"For a long time my father and Mr Busby discussed my chances of making good in the game. They discussed such things as pay and benefits and a second career in case I failed as a footballer. They satisfied each other on such points, and then my father turned to me and said: 'It's up to you Duncan. Do you want to join United?'

"Of course I said 'Yes', there was never any real question that I wouldn't."

This for some reason or another is totally wrong. Firstly, Duncan was signed by United long before his sixteenth birthday on October 1st, as he was an amateur with United at the start of season 1952-53. Secondly, Matt Busby had already met the Edwards family and as I have mentioned earlier, there is no reference there to sign Duncan anywhere except in Duncan's own book.

To clarify things a little bit more, the Manchester Evening Chronicle of June 4th carries a few lines on recent schoolboy signings and amongst the names of the aspiring stars is Duncan Edwards.

Although a schoolboy, Duncan was already something of a personality in his home town. So much so, that when he signed for Manchester United he was accorded something of a rare honour. To mark his success as a schoolboy footballer, a special subscription fund was opened with schoolboys and girls contributing towards a silver cup, which was to be known as the 'Duncan Edwards' trophy, which would be competed for on an annual basis.
At the inauguration of this special trophy, Duncan was presented with a replica of the cup.

The immediate post war years saw football go through something of a transitional period. Many player's had seen their careers come to a premature end due to injuries (and even death) brought about by the hostilities of the Second World War. Others, found that age was now against them forcing them to retire or step down a few levels if they wanted to continue playing the game they loved.

Club's around the country had relied heavily on guest players during the War League competitions and for many, on the resumption of League football in 1946, it was like starting from scratch. Taking Manchester United as an example, this can be seen from the difference in line ups from the League fixture against Charlton Athletic prior to the abandonment of League football in September 1940 and the first after the war against Grimsby Town on August 31st 1946.

Against Charlton, it read ... Breedon, Redwood Griffiths, Warner Chilton Whalley, Bryant Wassall Asquith Pearson and Wrigglesworth. Whilst the following faced Grimsby.......Crompton, Carey McGlen, Warner Chilton Cockburn, Delaney Pearson Hanlon Rowley and Mitten.
Having taken over Manchester United on February 19th 1945, Matt Busby had recognised the need for forward planning, especially when taking into consideration the ages of the players he had inherited. He had also noted, with much interest, upon his arrival that club that the chairman, James Gibson and secretary Walter Crickmer, had been instrumental in the setting up of the MUJAC's – the Manchester United Junior Athletic Club in 1938. Although not officially connected to United, all the facilities and coaches were made available to this new organisation.

The idea behind the MUJAC's was to provide local youngsters with the opportunity of playing in organised local football league's, while also bringing any talented local players to United's attention.
Busby, proceeded to take this idea one step further and relied on an experienced team of scouts to bring the best young players, not just in Manchester but from the country as a whole, to United. Between 1948 and 1950, the likes of David Pegg from Doncaster, Jackie Blanchflower from Belfast, Colin Webster from Cardiif, Mark Jones from Barnsley, Bill Foulkes from St.Helens and Manchester lads Jeff Whitefoot, Denis Viollet and Albert Scanlon were amongst those signed by the club on amateur forms. Oh, and of course the most recent one to put pen to paper, Duncan Edwards from Dudley.

On Monday June 9th 1952, Duncan said goodbye to his parents and boarded the train for Manchester. Much to his relief, however, he had company on the journey north, as his schoolboy international team mate Gordon Clayton, a native of nearby Cannock, had also recently signed for United, so there was much conversation between the two youngsters as to what lay ahead as the train chugged its way north.

The Black Country duo were met at Manchester's London Road Station by Bert Whalley, who took them to their new 'home', Mrs Watson's at 5 Birch Avenue, near to the Lancashire County Cricket ground. A short walk of course from United's Old Trafford stadium. Mrs Watson's was a large house, two actually knocked into one, and also home for other United youngsters such as Jackie Blanchflower, Mark Jones and David Pegg.

Life at United was not, however, all football. Before putting pen to paper, Duncan on instructions from his mentor Eric Booth had decided that if by any chance he did not make the grade then he needed something to fall back on and it was decided that he would take on an apprenticeship in carpentry. So, two days after arriving in Manchester, Duncan began his second career, with hammer, chisel and saw instead of the normal football boots. Although he was later to confess that he "hated" this part of being a junior footballer, he persevered with it until the day that he turned professional.

The United players reported back for training towards the end of July and by then, Duncan had settled in quietly to his new environment, longingly watching the clock as he toiled with his carpentry, whilst training with the junior players on Tuesday and Thursday evenings, for a couple of hours, at the Cliff in Lower Broughton.

Season 1952-53 kicked off for both United's senior professionals and the juniors with the official club practice matches at Old Traford – the Reds versus the Blues. Such fixtures were a common curtain raiser for the season ahead and were also popular with the supporters. Not only did it give them two games for the price of one, it also allowed the dedicated United supporter an early look at whatever new signings had been made during the close season.

The afternoon's highlight was obviously the first team versus the reserves, providing a highly competitive match with the second string eager to put one over those who were regarded as the first choice. But equally entertaining was the junior members of the playing staff own Reds versus Blues battle, as the new additions set out to create an early impression. It was obviously in this latter fixture that Duncan took part, enjoying his first game on the hallowed Old Trafford turf.

...‟I think all who saw the United juniors in action last Saturday will appreciate that we have some of the greatest youngsters in the country"...

For the record, Duncan turned out for the Reds and played his part in a pleasing 5-0 win. The two teams lined up as follows, Reds – Clayton, Fulton Bent, Whitehurst Cope Edwards, Morton McFarlane Hamilton Bradshaw and Pegg. The Blues – O'Gorman, Kennedy Rhodes, Evans (sub Colman) Taylor Barratt, Birkett Chapman (sub Lowrie) Lewis Doherty and Scanlon. The five Blues goals coming from Bradshaw 3 and McFarlane 2 and in one very brief match report the comment "the Reds half back line proved too strong for the Blues", is the only hint as to how Duncan faired in his first United outing.

In the club programme, the "United Review" for the opening match of the season against Chelsea, Matt Busby commented ..."I think all who saw the United juniors in action last Saturday will appreciate that we have some of the greatest youngsters in the country. I am not going to individualise, but I do think we can feel delighted with the success of all the junior stars. Here are names with which to conjure, and a few years hence we shall, no doubt, be ready to welcome to-days juniors as members of our senior side."

Tom Jackson, the Manchester Evening News United correspondent continued on the managers theme in his own programme notes, writing, ".....on the credit side, however, there are many new names in United's list of 'promising juniors'. They include schools internationals Gordon Clayton, a six foot goalkeeper from Cannock, Duncan Edwards left half back and captain of England Boys from Dudley, Alan Morton right winger from Tyneside and Alan Rhodes wing half from Chesterfield. Colin Webster, a Welsh boy who has scored a lot of goals at centre forward with RAF teams, youth international Walter Whitehurst left half from Ryder Brow and Brian Lowry inside forward from Manchester Boys are other newcomers whose names should be heard aplenty in the near future."

Duncan's competitive season got under way on August 23rd, playing for the Colts, in the Manchester Amateur League Division One, against Heywood St James at the Cliff training ground. Goals once again flowed freely, with the United youngsters winning 6-1. The United team read – O'Gorman Tucker Kennedy, Harrop Robbins Edwards, Dervin Humphries Hamilton Wood and Scanlon. Goals coming from Hamilton, Humphries and Wood, each scoring two a piece.

In the Colts' following two outings, against Roebuck Lane on August 27th and Dukinfield Town on August 30th, both away, Duncan continued in the No.6 jersey as 3-1 victories on both occasions were recorded, however, he was missing from the return against Roebuck Lane on September 1st.

Five days later, he was again missing from the Colts XI as they lined up at the Cliff against Platt Sports, but could be found quite a few miles away at Leek, turning out for the A team against Ball Haye Green, in what was a Manchester League fixture. Early promotion. The United team read – Clayton, Foulkes Bent, Whitehurst Robbins Edwards, Olive McFarlane Ritchie Doherty and Scanlon, with the goals in the closely fought 4-3 win coming from Ritchie 2, Olive and McFarlane.

As the weeks and months progressed, Duncan found himself drifting between the Colts and the A team, lining up against opposition such as Ferranti and Adelphi Lads. On October 10th, however, the competition and standard of opposition changed considerably with the United youngsters playing their initial match in the newly inaugurated F. A. Youth Cup.

The draw for the 1st round of the junior version of the F. A. Cup gave United a home draw against Leeds United and it was a proud Duncan Edwards who lead his team mates out onto the familiar Cliff training ground in Lower Broughton, Salford.

OCTOBER 10TH LEEDS UNITED H 4-0 FA YOUTH CUP 1ST ROUND

The teenage footballers from the other side of the Pennines were no match for their Lancastrian counterparts and inspired by the dynamic presence of Duncan Edwards within their ranks, the Manchester United youngsters encountered few problems in their 4-0 victory.
Although not amongst the goal scorers in this initial triumph, those coming from Albert Scanion with two, David Pegg and an own goal from a certain Jack Charlton, Duncan was very much involved for the duration of the ninety minutes.
It seems as though no area of the familiar Cliff Pitch would be left without the imprint of Duncan's studs, as he prompted his forwards and supported his defence, causing the Leeds side numerous problems.

Duncan was in his element under the glare of some what primitive floodlights compared to todays, providing the scattering of spectators a taste of what was to come in the Youth Cup competition.

Playing in the A team and in the F. A. Youth Cup provided Duncan with a slightly more competitive edge and his performances helped take the Manchester League side into second place in the table by the end of October, 4 points behind Taylor Bros. And 2 points in front of Miles Platting, having played, however, two games more. What brief mentions there were of the action from the often spartan playing fields which housed such fixtures revealed that the Dudley youngster was progressing well and his contributions made him a tremendous asset to the team. The one aspect of his game, however, that was perhaps in need of a boost was his goal scoring, as no matter how he tried, he just could not get his name on the score sheet.

Perhaps he had not been trying quite hard enough, as the second round of the F. A. Youth Cup saw him make up for all the previously scorned opportunities by hitting five in United's overwhelming 23-0 victory over an unfortunate Nantwich side.

The score line in itself attracted the headlines, but even it was over shadowed by Duncan's performance in the humiliation of the bewildered Cheshire side. "The greatest junior prospect I have ever seen. That is no exaggeration", wrote one reporter who was at the match, while another, Edgar Turner, penned the following.

"He is big and almost as strong as a man and I cannot recall one pass, long or short, by Edwards that could not be described to conjure up a phrase from the past such as a daisy cutter.

"His delivery of the ball to his forwards, even from well back, was equal to the best I have seen anywhere, league games and internationals included, for a very long time.

"When I say his tackling was strong and his covering excellent it is still not the end of the story. He also scored five goals!"

..."I am sure Matt Busby could give him a game in the first team now"

Further progress was made in this competition on the 26th of November when Bury, who certainly put up more resistance than the opponents of the previous round were defeated 2-0, with Duncan scoring the opening goal after only six minutes. Edgar Turner, who had witnessed the victory over Nantwich and enthused about Duncan's performance made sure he attended the 3rd round tie and although slightly disappointed in the reduced score line, again found pleasure in the youngsters display, witnessed another of his goals and within his report wrote .."I am sure Matt Busby could give him a game in the first team now".

Such minor fixtures rarely received much media coverage out with the local newspapers, so it was something of a surprise for United supporters to discover a sizeable report on a friendly, played at the Cliff on December 3rd against top amateur side Northern Nomads, in the Manchester Guardian. Within the column inches devoted to the match action was contained the following – "The encouraging thing

b. Edwards

AMENDED AGREEMENT

An Agreement made the Twelth

day of ___April,___ 19 55 between ___Walter___

___Crickmer,___ of ___Old Trafford,___

___Manchester,___ in the COUNTY OF ___Lancashire___

the Secretary of and acting pursuant to Resolution and Authority for and on

behalf of the ___MANCHESTER UNITED___ FOOTBALL CLUB

of ___MANCHESTER___ (hereinafter referred to as the Club)

of the one part and ___Duncan Edwards___

of ___2, Barlow Road, Stretford,___

in the County of ___Lancashire___ Professional Football Player

(hereinafter referred to as the Player) of the other part **Whereby** it is

agreed as follows :—

1. The Player hereby agrees to play in an efficient manner and to the best of his ability for the Club.

2. The Player shall attend the Club's ground or any other place decided upon by the Club for the purposes of or in connection with his training as a Player pursuant to the instructions of the Secretary, Manager, or Trainer of the Club, or of such other person, or persons, as the Club may appoint. [This provision shall not apply if the Player is engaged by the Club at a wage of less than One Pound, or at a wage per match.]

3. The Player shall do everything necessary to get and keep himself in the best possible condition so as to render the most efficient service to the Club and will carry out all the training and other instructions of the Club through its representative officials.

4. The Player shall observe and be subject to all the Rules, Regulations, and Bye-Laws of The Football Association, and any other Association, League, or Combination of which the Club shall be a member. As to all matters which shall be subject to any action which shall be taken by The Football Association under their Rules for the suspension or termination of this Agreement, the decision of such suspension or termination shall be decided upon by The Football Association, and likewise be suspended or terminated, as the case may be.

5. The Player shall not engage in any business or live in any place which the Directors (or Committee) of the Club may ...

9. In consideration of the observance by the said player of the terms, provisions and conditions of this Agreement, the said ___Walter___

___Crickmer___ on behalf of the Club hereby agrees that the said

Club shall pay to the said Player the sum of ___£8. 0. 0d___ per week from

___7th May, 1955.___

and £ _____ to ___30th June, 1955.___

to _____ per week from _____

10. This Agreement (subject to the Rules of The Football Association) shall cease and determine on ___30th June, 1955.___ unless the same shall have been previously determined in accordance with the provisions hereinbefore set forth.

Fill in any other provisions required.

As Witness the hands of the said parties the day and year first aforesaid

Signed by the said ___Walter___

___Crickmer___ and ___Duncan___

___Edwards___

In the presence of

(Signature) ___L. Olive___

(Occupation) ___Asst. Secy.___

(Address) ___21, London Street,___

___Salford, 5.___

Duncan Edwards (Player).

(Secretary).

THE CARPENTER FROM DUDLEY

about the game was that it showed a player of real promise in Edwards aged 16. He is remarkably fast, and tackled well, but best of all shot with real power with either foot. Even Rowley would not have criticised several of Edwards' drives for strength and direction".

Duncan's performance was noted by not only the scribe from the Guardian and the couple of thousand spectators at the game, but by the United officials at the game. So much so, that a couple of days later when Duncan checked the team lists for the weekend fixtures he found to his dismay that he was omitted from the A team, but moments later was surprised to find his name included in the Central League team for the first time.

So, December 6th brought yet another landmark in the footballing career of Duncan Edwards with his reserve team debut at Burnley. Unfortunately, he could not mark his debut with a win, as the home team were the scorers of the solitary goal which settled the game. He notched up a second Central League outing the following week against Preston North End at Old Trafford, helping United to a 2-1 victory, but was soon to find him back at grass roots level and amongst his friends in the 'A' team. By February, however, he had graduated to the Central League side on a permanent basis and had put together good run of appearances.

Progress had also been made in the FA Youth Cup, with the United youngster's now in round five thanks to a solitary goal by Duncan in round four against Everton on February 4th. Not renowned for scoring simple goals, this was another for the scrapbook. From a corner, he trapped and hit the ball all in one movement, with the Everton 'keeper rooted to the spot.

Three days later, on February 7th, following many near misses, the name of Duncan Edwards finally appeared on the score sheet, breaking his Central League duck with a goal on his own doorstep practically, at Molineux home of Wolverhampton Wanderers. Surprisingly, with the talent at their disposal, United's second string were fifth bottom of the Central League, some thirteen points behind third place Wolves.

"go and get your boots as you are playing in the first team tomorrow against Cardiff City"

The home side took the lead in the twenty-second minute, while playing with virtually ten men, following an injury to their centre forward. Despite this, it was not until nine minutes after the interval that United managed to get back onto level terms, with Duncan celebrating his first goal at this level. Pushing forward, a long ball out of defence found him running through the Wolves defence and from a narrow angle he shot home.

Unfortunately, it wasn't enough to secure a share of the points, as Wolves scored a second and what was to prove the winner, three minutes later.

For someone who loved his football, Duncan must have thrived on the number of games and the different standards of football in which he was involved during his first season with United. From the

Colts, to the A team, to the reserves and back to the Youth team, filling a variety of positions, he would have been in his element. However, as his first season moved towards its climax, with United out of contention for any of the major honours, he was in for a very unexpected summons to Matt Busby's office, as he carried out his normal tedious ground staff duties around the stadium. Wondering what he had done, that was serious enough for the boss wanting to see him, it was a nervous youngster who knocked rather timidly on his managers office door.

Entering, very much like a schoolboy summoned to his headmasters study, he was soon put at ease by the genial Scotsman, who quietly told him "go and get your boots as you are playing in the first team tomorrow against Cardiff City".

Sitting open mouthed, Duncan could not believe what he had just heard. He had never expected to achieve anything like first team level during his initial season at the club and although tremendously ambitious it was still something of a shock to be making such a big step up so soon.

"Don't say I said so, but this boy Edwards is the finest thing on two legs"

Obviously thrilled, he took the news calmly and upon regaining his composure asked the smiling Matt Busby if he could use his telephone to let his parents know the news. He then made his departure from the inner sanctions of the stadium and raced the few hundred yards down the road to give "Ma" Watson, "the best landlady anyone could wish for" and several other United youngsters the good news.

Upon receiving the unexpected telephone call at their Dudley home, Mr and Mrs Edwards immediately Made plans to travel to Old Trafford the following day. His father commented, "We are as excited as a couple of kids. In fact, Duncan is the calmest member of the family just now. He is used to playing before big crowds".

Busby, had already given four other youngsters their first team debuts this season – John Scott, Eddie Lewis, David Pegg and John Doherty, but what made the selection of Duncan Edwards a little different, was the fact that he was only 16 years old and still an amateur.

Surprisingly, an appraisal of the latest United debutante had appeared in the 'News Chronicle' on April 1st, when George Follows penned the following. "Like the father of the first atom bomb, Manchester United are waiting for something tremendous to happen. This tremendous football force they have discovered is Duncan Edwards, who is exactly sixteen and a half this morning.
"Though nobody can tell exactly what will happen when Edwards explodes into First Divison football, one thing is certain, it will be spectacular.
"Take these two testimonials from chief coaches of other clubs' after a recent Youth Cup game,
"Don't say I said so, but this boy Edwards is the finest thing on two legs".
"Don't say I said so, but this boy Edwards has got the lot".
What can you expect to see in Edwards?

Well, the first important thing is that this boy Edwards is a man of 12st. and 5ft 10 in. in height. That gives him his first great asset of power.

When he heads the ball, it is not a flabby flirtation with fortune, it is bold and decisive. When he tackles, it is with a man trap bite, and when he shoots with either foot, not even Jack Rowley – the pride of Old Trafford is shooting harder.

Add to this, body swerve and bravery and the sixth sense in a tight corner that distinguishes the truly great player and you have 'the boy who has the lot'.

If you think this is a lot to write about a lad of 16, I can only say "you obviously haven't seen this boy Edwards".

As the clock ticked towards three o'clock on Saturday April 4th, the home dressing room at Old Trafford was a hive of activity as the United players prepared to face Cardiff City. Duncan got changed quietly and pulled the red number six jersey over his already muscular frame as the team were called to take the field.

He was later to comment, "the thought of making my Football League debut was not terrifying, after having played at Wembley three times before I was 15".

"The only ray of sunshine that filtered through the United gloom, was the display of boy debutante Duncan Edwards..."

APRIL 4TH CARDIFF CITY H 1-4

For the collector of football memorabilia, it is disappointing that the name of Duncan Edwards does not appear in the 'United Review' covering this match due to print deadlines, but the 37,163 spectators were well aware who the debutante was without the need of a programme.

Those who were not at the game were made well aware of the prodigy's initial appearance as the newspapers were quick to mention his contribution to what was sadly not the best of United performances.

"The only ray of sunshine that filtered through the United gloom, was the display of boy debutante Duncan Edwards, who did all that was asked of him, including taking a shot from 30 yards that was only just wide", wrote Alf Clarke of the Manchester Evening Chronicle.

In the Manchester Guardian, their correspondent wrote –"He had the misfortune for this to be his first senior game. He showed promise of fine ability in passing and shooting but will have to move faster as a wing half. However, he cannot be judged on this match".

Frank Taylor, in the News Chronicle echoed the words of his press box associates, but hinted that he thought the youngster "looked a bit thick around the hips".

When looking back at this sixteen year olds' debut, it should be noted that three days previously he had been lining up in the United 'A' team for a Gilgryst Cup Final at the Cliff training ground against Ashton United.

..."If I thought that I was certain of seeing Duncan Edwards give another such polished display as he gave last night, wild horses would not keep me from Molineux..."

The following Saturday saw Duncan descend the footballing ladder to youth team level once again. Having progressed to the semi-final of the Youth Cup competition, they faced Brentford in the first leg at Griffin Park, where goals from McFarlane and Scanlon against a solitary home effort gave United a slight advantage to take north. The second leg, four days later was, however, a completely different story, much to the visitors disappointment.

By a strange co-incidence for Duncan, United's opponents in the Final were his local club, Wolverhampton Wanderers. In the May 4th first leg at Old Trafford, the United youngsters overwhelmed their Midland opponents, as they had other teams in previous weeks, recording a 7-1 win. Goals from Lewis 2, McFarlane 2, Pegg, Scanlon and Whelan thrilling the 20,934 crowd.

Even the Wolverhampton Express and Star correspondent who covered the match was impressed, writing under the heading 'Dudley Boy the Inspiration in Manchester United's Youth Cup Lead': "If I thought that I was certain of seeing Duncan Edwards give another such polished display as he gave last night, wild horses would not keep me from Molineux. Edwards, was to all intents and purposes the complete wing half back.

Strong man in a strong side, he failed only once in the whole game to make good use of the ball and if for nothing else, I would remember him for the uncanny accuracy of a series of long raking passes across the field on the inside of the full back, not to mention the urgency with which he played throughout.

Back on their own patch, the Wolves lads felt slightly more comfortable with their opponents, which showed in the 2-2 score line. It was not enough, however, to prevent the FA Youth Cup from becoming pride of place in Matt Busby's office at Old Trafford.

CHAPTER THREE
THE REPLACEMENT BECOMES A REGULAR

Having enjoyed his initial taste of First Division football, Duncan looked forward to season 1953-54 in the hope that he would be considered worthy of selection again at some point in the weeks and months ahead.

The experienced players, such as John Aston, Allenby Chilton, Henry Cockburn, Jack Rowley and Stan Pearson, who had been instrumental in the recent successes at the club, were still commanding first team places. Duncan, although ambitious, also realised that he had time on his side and if he continued to progress that sought after first team place would come his way. In the meantime, as long as he was playing football he was happy.

For countless junior players at clubs' up and down the country, the weeks leading up to their 17th birthday was something of a nerve-racking time, with the constant worry over whether or not they would be offered a professional contract. United youngster extraordinaire, Duncan Edwards had no worries in that respect. A professional contract was duly produced from Matt Busby's desk drawer on October 1st and a signature was quickly scribbled in the relevant space. A dream had been fulfilled.

Five days previously, Duncan had found himself omitted from the United Central League side, where he had been in fine form since playing a major part in the opening day 3-2 victory over Liverpool. There was no disappointment though, except that he would be spending a Saturday afternoon without kicking a ball, as he was named as 12th man for the first team's visit to White Hart Lane to face Tottenham Hotspur. He was happy to resume his reserve team duty's three days later, as it meant competitive involvement not inactivity as a spectator, something that he did not enjoy.

Having helped his team-mates lift the F.A. Youth Cup last season, there was excitement in the air when the draw for the first round of this season's competition was made, pairing United with Everton. A solitary goal, scored by Eddie Colman, took United through, in what was a closely fought ninety minutes. The Salford born goalscorer had become a great friend of Duncan's, making them something of an odd pair. The local lad being small in stature compared to the colossus from the West Midlands. Both, however, had been noted as exceptional individuals with promising futures.

On October 28th, four days after the Youth Cup victory, Duncan found himself once again travelling with the first team, heading northwards to Scotland for a floodlight friendly against Kilmarnock. Much to his disappointment, he once again found himself sitting on the touchline as the action was played out in front of him. On this occasion, his disappointment was to be short lived.

United's Ayrshire hosts found themselves a goal behind after only three minutes, through a rare Henry Cockburn effort, the England internationalist finding the net with a fine shot from 20 yards out. The satisfaction of scoring such a fine goal, despite the match being a mere friendly, was short lived, as the United half back suffered an injury shortly afterwards and was forced to leave the pitch.

Fortunately for United, and more so for Duncan Edwards, it had been agreed before hand to use substitutions if an injury occurred. The young wing half was an ideal replacement and following a quick warm up on the cinder track at the side of the pitch, he was on for a rare first team outing.

The 16,000 home supporters were given little to shout about as the match continued, with United assuming control, scoring another two goals, through Viollet and Taylor, thus ending an enjoyable few days on the west coast of Scotland.

United's season had began in something of a disappointing fashion, winning only four of their opening fifteen games, six of the others having been drawn. Matt Busby had obviously been concerned by the poor start and by what he had seen. He had also been contemplating making changes to his somewhat ageing side. With an away trip to Huddersfield Town pending, he decided to keep Jackie Blanchflower and Dennis Viollet in the side following their promising displays against Kilmarnock, with Duncan retaining the number six jersey in place of the injured Cockburn, giving the side a rather youthful look.

OCTOBER 31ST HUDDERSFIELD TOWN A 0-0

"Busby's Bouncing Babes Keep All Town Awake" proclaimed the headlines in the Manchester Evening Chronicle, thus creating a nickname that would vibrate around the world in the weeks, months and years ahead.
The three youngster's, Dennis Viollet, Jackie Blanchflower and Duncan adapted well to the change of pace in the First Division fixture and in the case of the latter, the longer the game went on, the more he came into it. Many observers particularly noted his stamina for one so young.

"Busby's Bouncing Babes Keep All Town Awake"

As the second half progressed, an opportunity to break the deadlock between the two teams fell to Duncan when a neat back pass from Tommy Taylor sent him racing for goal. Unfortunately his shot, while on target, lacked pace and a defender was able to clear.

NOVEMBER 7TH ARSENAL H 2-2

Retained his place in the United line up and the doyen of 1950's football writers, Don Davies, who wrote under the pen name of 'An Old International' wrote the following in his 'Guardian' match report –
'Edwards at left half showed uncanny judgement and maturity for a boy of seventeen. His tackling was strong, his ball play faultless and he alone was rarely at fault in following Rowley's promptings'.
Other reports noted that Duncan also came close to scoring on a couple occasions, one deflected off a defender for a corner, while another, from 25 yards went just wide.

NOVEMBER 14TH CARDIFF CITY A 6-1

United were in devastating form against the Welsh side, two goals up in the opening 4 minutes. Duncan, along with wing half partner Jeff Whitefoot contributed a clever and constructive display to which Cardiff had no answer.

NOVEMBER 21ST BLACKPOOL H 4-1

With a team containing seven players under the age of 21, a Matthews less Blackpool were well beaten by United.
There was no meeting between Duncan and his former boarding house host from his schoolboy days, but he did find himself up against the highly experienced Ernie Taylor. The Blackpool man opened strongly, but soon found himself being played out of the game, as the United wing half displayed shrewdness and fine judgement as his opponent found it more and more difficult to become involved in the running of the game. This did prove that old heads could indeed grow on young shoulders.
There were a few present who wondered, however, if there was such a thing as beginners luck!

NOVEMBER 28TH PORTSMOUTH A 1-1

With seven player's aged 21 or under, United stole a point despite a strong defensive display by Portsmouth.
The home side went a goal in front five minutes before half time as the United youngsters struggled to get into the game. To their credit, they persevered and succeeded in breaching the Portsmouth rearguard in the 70th minute with a goal from Tommy Taylor.

DECEMBER 5TH SHEFFIELD UNITED H 2-2

A rough-house of a game, with Sheffield's tactics clearly designed to upset the young United side. Fortunately Duncan did not get dragged into this physical confrontation. The referee did speak him to on one occasion though, for upending Wragg.

DECEMBER 12TH CHELSEA A 1-3

United's first defeat in eight games.
Despite being a goal behind at half time, United still looked capable of snatching something from the game. Their hopes were completely dashed when the home side increased their advantage in the 54th and 62nd minutes, giving them an unassailable lead.

DECEMBER 19TH LIVERPOOL H 5-1

Another exhilaration home team performance against bottom of the table Liverpool, with the artistry of Whitefoot and the strength of Duncan of particular note. For the first time at senior level, Duncan was unanimously considered the outstanding player on the pitch.

DECEMBER 25TH SHEFFIELD WEDNESDAY H 5-2
DECEMBER 26TH SHEFFIELD WEDNESDAY A 1-0

It was certainly not a happy Christmas for the Sheffield Wednesday players and supporters, as United took all four points from their Christmas Day and Boxing Day meetings.
A Tommy Taylor hat trick and further goals from Jackie Blanchflower and Dennis Viollet gave Wednesday little to cheer about at Old Trafford in their 5-2 defeat. However, an improved Wednesday performance in front of their own supporters the following day saw United slightly subdued.
On this occasion, a Dennis Viollet goal was all that separated the two sides.

JANUARY 2ND NEWCASTLE UNITED A 2-1

Once again, Duncan came close to opening his goal scoring account and it was Tommy Taylor who was again the provider. Turning the ball back to his wing half, Duncan quickly brought the ball under control before hitting a great right foot drive which travelled at terrific speed along the ground, forcing Simpson to make a splendid save.
Duncan was always alert to such opportunities and was as confident going forward as he was defending. A second effort, from just outside the box, had the beating of Simpson but went wide of the Newcastle 'keepers post.

JANUARY 9TH BURNLEY A 3-5 F.A. CUP 3rd ROUND

Duncan's first F.A. Cup tie and it proved to be something of a disappointment, with the home side recording an emphatic victory against their Lancashire neighbours. Burnley opened the scoring in the 2nd minute, adding a second three minutes later. Not to be outdone, United stunned their hosts by drawing level with two goals in as many minutes. 2-2 and only seven minutes played!
Burnley again took the lead in the 18th minute, with United equalising in the 52nd. The home side's

..."But for me, the final memory will be of the boy Edwards striding through the mud in hopeless battle, the bravest man on the field"

determination eventually proved superior and two further goals were enough to put the tie beyond United's grasp. In the post match debates, many queried Matt Busby's team selection of including five youngsters.

Although the youngest player on the park, Duncan gave a creditable performance and in his summary of the match, George Follows of the 'Daily Herald' wrote.....'But for me, the final memory will be of the boy Edwards striding through the mud in hopeless battle, the bravest man on the field".

Duncan had by now notched up a run of twelve consecutive appearances in the Manchester United first team, keeping the now fully fit Henry Cockburn on the sidelines, much to the seasoned campaigners disappointment. So much so that Cockburn asked to be put on the transfer list, as he felt that at his stage of his career he had to be playing first team football.

Henry Cockburn held no animosity against the youngster keeping him out of the United side, in fact he went out of his way to help and encourage the player who could be considered his understudy. Before games, he would sit down with Duncan and go through the opposition player by player, pointing out the danger men and their particular strengths.

Although Henry Cockburn's transfer request was at this particular time turned down, he was eventually allowed to leave the club, joining Oldham ten moths later.

JANUARY 16TH MANCHESTER CITY H 1-1

Seven days after his first F.A.Cup tie came Duncan's first Manchester 'derby', with neighbours City visiting Old Trafford. Unmoved by the occasion and the vociferous 46,379 crowd he was clearly United's man of the match. Covering every inch of the Old Trafford pitch, he checked numerous City attacks and continually prompting his own forwards.

He did receive some criticism though and was blamed for the City goal and also for neglecting his left wing team mate David Pegg, while happy to send passes over to the opposite flank and through to centre forward Tommy Taylor.

His enthusiasm and determination was not, however, matched by his team mates and their rivals were happy to back across the city to Maine Road with a point.

While only a boy in a man's world and really a novice at this level of football, the name of Duncan Edwards was already on everyones lips, with many even going as far as to suggest that he should be considered as a possible candidate for a place in the full England side for forthcoming internationals.

The England selectors were well aware of his ability and his name had been noted as a future full international prospect. In the meantime, Duncan had to be content with selection for the under 23 side to face Italy in Bologna, the first of its kind at this level, on January 20th.

In years to come, Duncan would admit to his dislike of flying and it was perhaps the outward flight to Bologna, which prompted this. The flight out on the day before the match saw many of the England team suffer from air-sickness, Duncan included, preventing proper preparation for the match ahead. This was to show in the performances of many and the subsequent result. Italy under 23's 3 - England under 23's 0.

JANUARY 23RD BOLTON WANDERERS H 1-5

Having suffered defeat in the F.A.Cup at the hands of near neighbours Burnley, United suffered another five goal humiliation against Lancashire opposition, in what was described as their worst display in years. While Duncan, and his United colleagues struggled through the afternoon, his former England schools team mate Ray Parry had an excellent game for the visitors, scoring twice.

Whilst now a first team regular, it must be remembered that the seventeen year old was still eligible to play in the United Youth team, who had by now progressed to the fifth round of the national competition with emphatic 5-0 and 6-0 victories against Wrexham and Bradford in rounds two and three respectively. Surprisingly after those two high scoring victories, they had failed to find the net in round four, being held to a goal less draw at Rotherham.

"It was my first glimpse of Duncan Edwards and indeed he is an amazing player..."

On January 27th in the replay at the Cliff, the Rotherham lads were in for something of a treat – ninety minutes in the company of Duncan Edwards, who had been drafted into the team. Despite their performance in the first game, the visitors had no answer to the 'new face' in the United line up and they were on the end of a 3-1 defeat, all the United goals coming from – Duncan Edwards!

In the 'South Yorkshire and Rotherham Advertiser' their man at the match wrote : "It was my first glimpse of Duncan Edwards and indeed he is an amazing player, almost of the John Charles stamp already. He was almost the entire reason for Manchester's supremacy, for not only did he score all their goals, but he also dominated the play throughout.
"I think it was a pity that Manchester, in their eagerness to make sure of retaining this cup, which they won last season, found it necessary to bring into the side Duncan Edwards, who played in the England under 23 side against Italy last week and has made twenty four First Division appearances. I know Edwards is only seventeen, but I think it is against the basics of the Youth Cup to introduce professional players."

FEBRUARY 6TH PRESTON NORTH END A 3-1

United warmed the blood on a freezing cold afternoon with three goals in the opening 24 minutes. They got off to an excellent start with Blanchflower scoring in the very first minute and despite the bone hard playing surface adapted well to the conditions scoring a further two goals before half time.
In the second forty five minutes, Preston tried to claw their way back into the game and play became rather physical. They eventually managed to pull one goal back in the 60th minute, but United remained in control and maintained their good record at Deepdale.

FEBRUARY 13TH TOTTENHAM HOTSPUR H 2-0

Reportedly one of his best games for United yet, as he was given the scope to play by the Londoners. Created one of United's two goals with a beautiful through pass, whilst having an effort of his own cleared off the line.

FEBRUARY 20TH BURNLEY A 0-2

A disappointing afternoon with numerous goalscoring opportunities going begging as the United forward line failed to click.
Burnley had opened their scoring account in the 12th minute and despite some good work by the United defence, it was not until a minute from time that increased their lead.

FEBRUARY 27TH SUNDERLAND A 2-0

The blizzard conditions and the snow covered pitch did little to prevent yet another quality performance. Although up against the talented, local favourite Len Shackleton, he found time to depart his defensive duties and create problems for the Sunderland defence with some astute passing. Due to the adverse weather conditions, the pitch cut up badly, but this proved to be of little hindrance to Duncan who plodded on as if it were a summer's afternoon.

MARCH 6TH WOLVERHAMPTON WANDERERS H 1-0

A fine defensive display by Wolves, springing the offside trap time and again, seemed to have been enough to earn them a point. But with five minutes left to play, their tactical plan let them down as Johnny Berry moving onto a Jackie Blanchflower pass, saw the linesman keep his flag down and the United winger ran through to score.

The fixtures for March 13th listed Aston Villa at home to Manchester United, but the name of Duncan Edwards was a surprise omission from the team that travelled to the Midlands for the match, giving

"...where's this great Edwards of yours?
We ain't seen him yet"

Henry Cockburn a very rare start. The reason for the non-appearance was quite simple, his services were required elsewhere, as the United youth team had a quarter final cup tie in Kent against Bexley Heath and Welling.

Some 8,000 spectators were attracted to the small compact ground, most hoping for a home win, but many simply wanting to see some of the names that had been brought to their attention in the national press.

The game opened relatively quietly with neither side gaining any real advantage and as the first half progressed the crowd became restless in the wait for the deadlock to be broken. Due to the proximity of the trainers bench to the crowd along the touch line, every moan, groan, complaint or whatever was clearly audible and with the game in something of a stalemate a voice echoed through the air – "Murphy, where's this great Edwards of yours? We ain't seen him yet".

On cue, as if he had heard the voice from the crowd, Duncan gathered the ball in the centre of the field, moved forward a few feet before sending the ball into the back of the Bexley Heath net with incredible power. Smiling, Jimmy Murphy turned to the crowd and said, "that, is Duncan Edwards".

To their credit, the home side played their way back into the game, equalising before the interval, but in the end found the United side just too strong and experienced, with David Pegg snatching a late winner.

MARCH 20TH HUDDERSFIELD TOWN H 3-1

Back in the first team, with Henry Cockburn stepping down. Made the second goal for Dennis Viollet.

Four days later, along with his United team mate and captain Roger Byrne, Duncan was on international duty, representing the England under 23 side in Gelsenkirchen against their German equivalents. The first post war international between the two countries. As one newspaper reported, "that in itself was significant, but what was also important was the inclusion of Duncan Edwards adding the most colourful chapter yet in his exciting and romantic story".

The German's had no answer to Duncan, never mind the rest of the visiting team and immediately took to the player that they found hard to believe was not yet eighteen, applauding him warmly throughout England's 4-0 win.

In his report of the game, Desmond Hackett of the 'Daily Express' wrote - " Already man sized and carrying a football brain to match, this Edwards is going to become the terror of the continent before he has even got down to serious shaving. He was certainly the despair of the Germans".

Another reporter, John Graydon of the Evening Chronicle, likened Duncan's build to that of a "Sherman tank" and compared him to being "as tough as Wilf Copping, the greatest of England's post war forwards". He also commented that " in Germany, his tackling put the continentals completely off their game and when he cleared the ball, he hit it really hard and accurately to his colleagues. If he gives a good game against Arsenal, he is favourite to be England's left half in the forthcoming match against Scotland".

MARCH 27TH ARSENAL A 1-3

Duncan had been widely tipped for a place in the England side for forthcoming internationals and with members of the England selection committee watching from the Highbury stand, it was rather unfortunate that Duncan should give what was perhaps his poorest performance of the season. He failed to become totally involved in the game, misplacing passes and making elementary errors which lead to Arsenal scoring two of their goals. His hopes of selection for the full England side were severely dashed. Fortunately time was still very much on his side.

APRIL 3RD CARDIFF CITY H 2-3

A rather poor and uninteresting display despite the five goals shared.
Cardiff certainly avenged their 6-1 defeat earlier in the season, overturning United's 2-0 lead, which they held with only fifteen minutes to go. Two goals in the final three minutes gave the Welsh side both points

APRIL 10TH BLACKPOOL A 0-2

A third consecutive defeat which saw Johnny Aston make a surprise return to the first team, more so because he was selected to play in the centre forward position. This was only his seventh start of the season.
Duncan enjoyed a favourable afternoon despite the score, coming face to face with Matthews on more than one occasion and always gaining the upper hand, earning a round of applause for one superb challenge on the England man.
Once again, the forwards let the rest of the team down.

APRIL 16TH CHARLTON ATHLETIC H 2-0

Back to their winning ways, in what was described as a "guileless, soulless and almost hopeless soccer match."
Goals from Viollet and Aston gave United both points, but it still left them 5th in the table, some eight points behind leaders Wolves.

APRIL 17TH PORTSMOUTH H 2-0

Something of a typical end of season game with nothing but pride to play for.
United's forward line continued to struggle at times and play became erratic by both sides. Duncan, although praised for the "immense amount of work" he was doing, was criticised also for being "distressingly inaccurate in his passing."

Duncan's League season came to an end with two games still to play, as his services were required elsewhere. The F.A. Youth Cup campaign had continued to roll along and the United lads had fought their way through to the Final for the second successive season, having beaten West Bromwich Albion in the semi final, 7-1 on aggregate. Their opponents in the Final, surprisingly enough were last seasons beaten finalists Wolverhampton Wanderers, presenting them with the opportunity of securing some sort of revenge.

In the first leg at Old Trafford, on April 23rd, the Midlands youngsters were certainly intent on wrestling the trophy from United's grasp, putting up a spirited and commendable display in a fiercely fought 4-4 draw.

Much to the astonishment of the majority of the 18,246 crowd, the visitors took a 3-1 first half lead, Duncan having scored United's solitary effort, which had in fact put them 1-0 in front. The second forty-five minutes, however, was an entirely different story, with Wolves pegged back in their own half of the pitch as United mounted attack after attack.

Duncan, who had begun the game at inside right, switched to centre forward and the game suddenly swung United's way. Scoring with a powerful header, he made it 3-2 and shortly afterwards David Pegg put the tie level. Wolves, to their credit, kept plodding away and somehow managed to score a fourth, but Pegg once again put the teams level. As the minutes ticked away, the visitors were well and truly on the defensive and happily kicked the ball anywhere to avoid conceding another goal.

Three days later, it was a familiar journey to the West Midlands for the Dudley born United teenager for a match, watched by 28,651 spectators, which was as closely contested as the previous encounter in Manchester.

Again, it was the local lad who was the thorn in the Wolverhampton side, moving between inside and centre forward, causing the home defence numerous problems and quite often taking three defenders to mark him.

With 33 minutes played, a high ball into the Wolves penalty area saw Duncan rise alongside two defenders. Colliding in mid-air, the defenders ended up sprawled on the ground, while Duncan landed comfortably on his feet. Much to the surprise and annoyance of the home support, the referee pointed to the penalty spot and David Pegg coolly placed the kick beyond the 'keeper to give United a 1-0 advantage. As it turned out, this was the only goal of the game and the trophy returned to Manchester with the bubbling bunch of freshly scrubbed faces in the United coach, enjoying their celebrationary bottles of lemonade.

"the most enjoyable match of my career to date"...
"the opposing forward line of Matthews, Mannion, Lawton, Shackleton and Langton certainly gave us the run-around, but I really enjoyed playing against such great players"

Despite his poor showing in front of the England selectors at Highbury back in March, Duncan was given the opportunity of redeeming himself and putting forward his case for selection at a later date, as it was now too late to hope for inclusion in the squad for the forthcoming World Cup in Switzerland. As something of a practice match, ironically played at Highbury, Duncan, along with team mates Roger Byrne Tommy Taylor and Dennis Viollet lined up for a Young England side in what was to become something of a regular fixture, played on April 30th, the eve of the F.A.Cup Final, against the senior England eleven.

Despite the senior side winning 2-1, Duncan later recalled the evening as "the most enjoyable match of my career to date". He went on to say, "the opposing forward line of Matthews, Mannion, Lawton, Shackleton and Langton certainly gave us the run-around, but I really enjoyed playing against such great players".

Although there was no last minute World Cup call up, Duncan did find himself on an aeroplane bound for Switzerland at the end of the season, heading with his United youth team mates for the prestigious Blue Star Youth tournament in Zurich. Such a competition gave Matt Busby the opportunity of comparing his stars of the future with those on the continent, but it was obvious to all, by the end of the 16 team tournament who was going to be the biggest star of all.

It was a proud United manager who watched his youngsters lift the trophy, winning four of their games and drawing the other without conceding a goal. In the Final itself, Red Star of Zurich were beaten 4-0, centre forward Duncan Edwards scoring a hat trick, with Albert Scanlon scoring the other.

Matt Busby wrote the following about the tournament in the Manchester Evening Chronicle – "I played Duncan Edwards in his normal position at left half in the first three games, although I moved him to centre forward for the later stages of the third game. In the semi-final and final, I played Edwards and he scored a magnificent hat trick in the Final".

Perhaps a bigger thrill for the United youths than winning the competition was playing a Swiss Youth select side in the national stadium prior to the Switzerland versus Holland full international. Needless to say, United won this match as well, 4-0, with goals from Pegg 2, Whelan and you've guessed it, Edwards.

So, at long last, the curtain came down on what had been a strenuous, but memorable season for Duncan Edwards. He could now head home to Dudley to spend some time with his parents, get his fishing rod out and see his old schoolboy friends, without having to live up to the expectations of the British footballing public.

CHAPTER FOUR
ENGLAND AND A GOAL, AT LAST

With so many of the Manchester United players around the same age and also living together in the same digs, it was not surprising that they also spent much of their leisure time in each others company. Friday night was usually a visit to the cinema to relax before the following days fixtures, while Saturday's would often mean the Locarno Ballroom in Sale or the Plaza in Manchester. Duncan certainly enjoyed the former, but at the latter, he was content to simply stand on the edge of the dance floor listening to the music. Surprising really when you recall his love for Morris and Sword dancing at school only a few years ago.

Duncan enjoyed the company of his United team mates and was always 'one of the gang', but he was only totally confident when he was playing football.

Refreshed from his summer break, Duncan headed back to 'Ma' Watson's, Old Trafford and pre season training. Due to the World Cup, season 1954-55 did not get under way until the second last week of August and following the Reds versus the Blues pre season curtain raiser at Old Trafford, the league campaign got under way with Portsmouth making the long journey up to Manchester.

AUGUST 21ST PORTSMOUTH H 1-3

A disappointing start to the season, with everyone in the United side turning in a below par performance as the visitors happily accepted their good fortune and returned home with three well earned points.

AUGUST 23RD SHEFFIELD WEDNESDAY A 4-2

As a team performance, it was certainly a big improvement from two days previously. However, much to Duncan's disappointment, he was responsible for one of the Sheffield Wednesday goals, upending Albert Quixall inside the area to give away a penalty kick.

AUGUST 28TH BLACKPOOL A 4-2

Another four goal victory and another much improved team performance, with Duncan keeping the home forwards in check for most of the ninety minutes.

Matt Busby's habit of taking one of the youngsters along with the first team as twelfth man, as he had done with Duncan, continued, with Eddie Colman enjoying his first away day with the seniors. Duncan and the fun loving Salford born Colman were great friends and the pair can be imagined on the team coach as it approached the seaside resort competing against each other to see who could spot the famous tower first!

SEPTEMBER 1ST SHEFFIELD WEDNESDAY H 2-0

Two first half Dennis Viollet goals, making it four in the two games against the Hillsborough side, gave United the points in front of a shirt sleeved Old Trafford crowd.

United should certainly have scored more due to the opportunities that they had, but the visitors got back into the game and it was only some good defensive work by the United half back line kept them at bay.

SEPTEMBER 4TH CHARLTON ATHLETIC H 3-1

Bartram in the Charlton goal saved his side from a much heavier defeat, as United turned on the style to remain equal with Everton at the top of the First Division.

Goals from Jack Rowley 2 and Taylor claimed the points, with Charlton claiming a late consolation goal in the last minute.

SEPTEMBER 8TH TOTTENHAM HOTSPUR A 2-0

Following yet another creditable performance, it was widely suggested that along with team mates Roger Byrne, Ray Wood and Dennis Viollet, selection for the full England side was something which would happen sooner rather than later.

SEPTEMBER 11TH BOLTON WANDERERS A 1-1

Bolton's best attendance of the season to date saw a keenly fought encounter with both defences well on top. Bolton thought that they had snatched a late winner in the 84th minute, but with only three minutes left to play, Colin Webster equalised.

SEPTEMBER 15TH TOTTENHAM HOTSPUR H 2-1

"Edward's Out On His Own" proclaimed the headlines in the Daily Dispatch and the report continued...." The youngest player on view, 17 year old Duncan Edwards, was the star of the match. He got through a tremendous amount of work and earned applause time and again, not only for his constructive work, but also for his defensive qualities".

He gave one of the best displays of wing half play we have seen at Old Trafford for years. Everything he did was accomplished with the ease and grace of a seasoned player".

"Edward's Out On His Own"

SEPTEMBER 18TH HUDDERSFIELD TOWN H 1-1

Duncan was developing a fine understanding alongside defensive stalwart Allenby Chilton and turned in a commanding display against the Yorkshire visitors. During the game he picked up a slight knee injury, but in typical fashion simply shrugged his shoulders and plodded on, working his way back into the game. Following this performance there was once again numerous voices suggesting that he should be given his first full England cap and with England selector Mr H.Shentall at Old Trafford for the second time in four days, rumours that such a honour was imminent were rife, especially in the Manchester area.

SEPTEMBER 25TH MANCHESTER CITY A 2-3

Following an eight game unbeaten run it was particularly annoying to loose it to neighbours City and it must have been a frustrating ninety minutes for Duncan. Not only did he have a poor afternoon, despite being in the thick of things, with many of his usual pinpoint passes going astray, he found himself get in the way of a shot from a City forward and could do nothing but stand and agonisingly watch as it deflected past Ray Wood, much to the delight of the City supporters in the 54,105 Maine Road crowd.

OCTOBER 2ND WOLVERHAMPTON WANDERS A 2-4

A change of position as he headed home to the Black Country to face Wolves, in what was to be a disappointing return. He played his part well at inside forward, but as he was settling into his new position, Allenby Chilton received an injury and was forced to leave the field, which meant that Duncan had to move back and take up the a defensive role in the heart of the defence.

OCTOBER 9TH CARDIFF CITY H 5-2

When Tommy Taylor completed his hat trick after 59 minutes, making the score line 3-1, the match, as a contest, was virtually over. For the second consecutive season, Cardiff were well beaten at Old Trafford.

OCTOBER 16TH CHELSEA A 6-5

An eleven goal thriller at Stamford Bridge, with United claiming both points with the odd goal. It was one of those games that come along only once every so often and every player played their part in a real crowd pleaser. Duncan battled in defence and aided the attack, but it was the United attacking force of Viollet, Taylor and Blanchflower who took the plaudits scoring three, two and one goal respectively.

Following the eleven goal, action packed ninety minutes against Chelsea, Duncan along with Roger Byrne and Ray Wood were off on international duty. It was, however, to no exotic or distant destination, but a few miles along the East Lancs. Road to Liverpool, as it was only a League international with the Irish League in opposition.

Despite the 4-2 score line, it was something of an uneventful game, with only the Football League half back line of Phillips, Wright and Edwards coming out of the game with any credit.

OCTOBER 23RD NEWCASTLE UNITED H 2-2

A game which kept the 29,217 crowd on their toes, as play flowed from end to end, with Chilton, ably assisted by Duncan, in outstanding form.

United went a goal down after only 16 minutes, but pulled back to lead 2-1 before Mitchell claimed an equaliser in the 70th minute.

OCTOBER 30TH EVERTON A 2-4

This is one game that Duncan Edwards would have wanted to forget, not for a poor performance, as over the ninety minutes, his was perhaps better than that of some of his team mates. He would not, however, have been too pleased at having scored two own goals, thus killing any hope that United had of salvaging something from the game.

In the 32nd minute he was penalised for a tackle from behind, while six minutes from time, with United fighting for an equaliser, he handled the ball inside the box.

NOVEMBER 6TH PRESTON NORTH END H 2-1

Dennis Viollet once again saved United's blushes with a couple of goals, making it 15 in 17 games, as Preston threatened to snatch at least a point in an exciting match at Old Trafford.

NOVEMBER 13TH SHEFFIELD UNITED A 0-3

A disappointing match from United's point of view. More than once, Duncan and his defensive colleagues had to be alert to prevent the home side from increasing their lead.

Although United tried hard, they failed to make the ball do the work for them.

On the 15th of November, Duncan travelled north to Scotland, something that was becoming a regular journey for him. United were due to face Hibernians at Easter Road, but manager Matt Busby decided to leave him out of the side to face the Scottish side. Busby also left him out of the United side to face Arsenal at Old Trafford on November 20th, due to the fact that along with team mate Gordon Clayton, they were due to play for the England Youth team against Holland Youth in Arnhem.

NOVEMBER 27TH WEST BROMWICH ALBION A 0-2

A second consecutive away defeat, under difficult playing conditions, saw United slip further down the table. Failing to take advantage of the wind and rain in the first half, they faced an uphill struggle in the second forty-five minutes.

Duncan returned to the side at left half in place of Freddie Goodwin, following his appearance for England Youths in Holland.

Since becoming a first team regular, Duncan had only been missing from First Division action when his talents were required elsewhere. The odd knocks here and there were commonplace with the type of game he played, but they were never enough to keep him sidelined and out of the starting line up.

He was, however, missing from the team who faced Leicester City at Old Trafford on December 4th, but it was no football inflicted injury that brought the omission, but a boil on his ankle. Fortunately, this cleared up sufficiently by the following week, but the first team had to once again do without his services at Burnley, on December 11th, as he was required to travel with the United youth team (for which he was yet again available) to Barnsley for a F.A. Youth Cup 3rd round tie.

The Yorkshire side must have been more than a little apprehensive upon learning of Duncan's inclusion in the United line up, as in the previous round at Maine Road, playing at centre forward, he had more or less taken on Manchester City's youth team single handedly, scoring both goals in a 2-1 victory.

One goal down at half time in that particular tie, on a real pea-souper of a foggy night, Jimmy Murphy showed some concern during the interval regarding the conditions and the score line, but was told "not

... "at centre forward, Duncan took control"...

to worry" by Duncan and he would see that everything went alright in the second forty five minutes. He did, as the match statistics show.

Against Barnsley, again at centre forward, Duncan took control, but as in the City match of the previous round it was only after the United youngsters found themselves behind.

Inspired by the sight of a First Division regular in the opposition ranks, the home side took the game to United and to their surprise and obvious delight went 2-0 in front. At half time, Jimmy Murphy's team talk must have been strong and to the point and his gruff Welsh tones certainly spurned the visitors into action. Barnsley found themselves immediately under pressure and like City, had no answer to the inspirational United number nine, who made three and scored one goal as United overturned the 2-0 half time deficit to win 4-2.

DECEMBER 18TH PORTSMOUTH A 0-0

Not for the first time this season, it was the United half back line that salvaged something from a game. On this occasion, it read Gibson, Chilton and Edwards who wore the no.4, 5 and 6 shirts. The game itself, was rather scrappy, but given the poor playing conditions the visiting defence coped well.

DECEMBER 27TH ASTON VILLA H 0-1
DECEMBER 28TH ASTON VILLA A 1-2

A disappointing festive period for Duncan and his team mates as Villa dominated both fixtures, taking all four points. The home defeat was especially disappointing as the 49,136 crowd witnessed the first reversal at Old Trafford since the opening day of the season.

JANUARY 1ST BLACKPOOL H 4-1

Any footballer would have been highly satisfied with newspaper reviews and reports which followed Duncan's performances for Manchester United. Duncan himself was well content with what he had achieved to date, but there was one thing missing from his all round game and that was a goal. No matter how hard he had tried, he just could not put the ball past the opposing goalkeeper. Very few ninety minutes went past without one of his shots hitting the 'keeper or a defender and bouncing clear, or rebounding off the post or cross bar, or simply going narrowly wide of the goal. The triumphant day, however, had at last came.

..."a blurred object which first soared over Farm's upraised arms then dipped suddenly and passed in under the crossbar"...

Perhaps the moment is best described by Don Davies (An Old International) of the Manchester Guardian - "By common consent, the outstanding incident of a somewhat desultory second half was the scoring of Edwards' first goal for United. Ever since he first pulled a red jersey over his muscular frame, this justy 17 year old has dreamt of one thing only; namely to smite a ball so hard that it either bursts in transit or defies the effort of any goalkeeper to intercept it. On Saturday, with about twenty minutes remaining for play, Edwards at last detected his opportunity.

"Darting forward, he put every ounce of his prodigious strength into the mighty, uninhibited swipe. There was a sharp crack of boot on leather - a veritable detonation, this - and a clearing of the atmosphere by a blurred object which first soared over Farm's upraised arms then dipped suddenly and passed in under the crossbar.

"A scene of great commotion followed. Spectators hugged each other, then threw their heads back and brayed their approval. Edwards leaped and gambolled like a soul possessed, until his adoring colleagues fell upon him and pinned him down with their embraces. Chilton too, a smiling Caius Marcius Carrolanus, raced upfield and patted the prodigy's head: 'That's my brave boy'.

"It was all very touching and not in the least bit spoiled when Perry broke away and scored for Blackpool".

JANUARY 8TH READING A 1-1 FA CUP 3RD ROUND

A very poor ninety minutes against their lesser Third Division opponents. The home side took the lead and much as United tried, little would go right for them. As the minutes began to tick away, Duncan was moved up field in the hope that he could conjure a goal, following the opening of his account the previous Saturday, but to no avail.

With five minutes to go, a draw was finally salvaged, much to everyone's relief, when Colin Webster managed to steer the ball home.

JANUARY 12TH READING H 4-1 FA CUP 3RD ROUND REPLAY

Having struggled against the Third Division side, who saw a glimmer of hope in the original tie when Chilton put through his own goal, United made no mistake in the Old Trafford replay. Goals from Webster 2, Viollet and Rowley proving too much for the visitors.

"Flower's and Edwards, restless and strong, both in the air and in the tackle, were the masters of midfield"

Life was becoming rather hectic for the soldier-cum-footballer, with the prospect of two games per week more a probability than a possibility.

Following the mid-week F.A.Cup replay and the postponement of the League fixture against Charlton at the Valley on January 15th, notification was received of his selection for the England under 23 side to play a return fixture against the Italians at Chelsea's Stamford Bridge ground.

The majority of those who played in the 3-0 defeat in Bologna were now no longer within the age limit for selection, so it was a very different and stronger looking England side who sought revenge in South London on January 19th.

Revenge it certainly was, as the Italians suffered a 5-1 defeat. In the 'Times', their football correspondent wrote - "Flower's and Edwards, restless and strong, both in the air and in the tackle, were the masters of midfield."

JANUARY 22ND BOLTON WANDERERS H 1-1

Despite being spoiled by some untidy play and numerous fouls, it was an enthralling fixture between the local rivals. Played on a rather muddy pitch, it was noted that compared with most of the players, Duncan was playing just as strongly at the end as he had been at the start.

JANUARY 29TH MANCHESTER CITY A 0-2 FA CUP 4TH ROUND

With City making the most of their home advantage, they threw everything into attack right from the first whistle and for long periods of the opening forty-five minutes United were pegged back in defence. Twice, Duncan was forced to come to the rescue, preventing certain goals, firstly with a header and secondly with an overhead kick on the goal line.

It came as no surprise when City eventually took the lead and the game swung further in their favour when Allenby Chilton was sent off with twenty minutes still to play. Duncan was immediately moved into the centre of defence, as United attempted to force an equaliser.

It was Duncan himself who came closest to an equaliser, heading over from close range, receiving some black looks from his team-mates, who considered it was an opportunity scorned.

To be honest, Duncan was playing like a man possessed, appearing all over the place, marshalling the defence, whilst the next minute pushing forward in attack. On one of his sally's forward, he was upended as he prepared to shoot, took the free kick himself, but could only watch in despair as his effort was cleared.

Despite his exertions, City snatched a second goal with only two minutes to go and the cup dream was over for yet another season.

FEBRUARY 5TH HUDDERSFIELD TOWN A 3-1

At Leeds Road, Duncan found himself wearing the number ten jersey and partnering his England schoolboy team mate David Pegg on the left flank, due to the unavailability of Dennis Viollet. It was a move that certainly paid off, as the left wing pairing scored two of United's three goals.

The left-sided triangle of Jeff Whitefoot, Duncan and David Pegg, began the game well and were soon causing the home team problems. It was the latter of the trio who opened United's scoring account following a fine move between Roger Byrne and Duncan, who made the telling pass for the winger to score.

It was Duncan, who added the second, gladly accepting the opportunity when the Huddersfield goalkeeper failed to hold a shot from Webster who had done well to bring the ball under control and manage a forceful shot on target. Celebrations this time were a little bit more subdued.

A minute later, the United number ten almost scored his second, but could only watch his shot go narrowly past the upright. Johnny Berry did add a third later on.

As the game progressed, Duncan was here there and everywhere with his weight and tremendous energy certainly proving a great boost to the United attack.

Yet another under 23 cap was collected for the Edwards' trophy cabinet on February 8th and a few more miles added to his journeying up and down the country. This time, the opponents were Scotland, in what was the first meeting between the two at this level, with game played at Clyde's Shawfield Stadium.

This was Duncan's second visit to the Glasgow ground, the first back in September, when some 11,000 spectators enjoyed a 4-1 victory to the local.

On this occasion, however, their would be no highland flings or whatever on the terraces and in the streets after the match, as the England XI showed little compassion to their hosts in a demoralising 6-0 victory.

Duncan began the game at left half, but shortly after the start centre forward Bobby Ayre dislocated his elbow and was forced to leave the field. As substitutes were permitted, the English officials quickly moved Duncan to centre forward and sent on Stan Anderson to fill the left half position. The move certainly did not weaken the team and if anything made it physically stronger, presenting a bigger challenge to the home side.

On the half hour, England's make shift centre forward was brought down just outside the penalty box. Haynes took the free kick, passing it a few feet to Bluntstone, who fired home to open the scoring. Shortly before the interval, Atteyo added a second.

The second forty five minutes certainly gave the crowd value for money, if it did not give them any pleasure, as Duncan took over the game with a devastating display, which left the Scottish defence demoralised and everyone talking about the player for days to come.

No sooner was the second half under way, when Duncan gave the Scots notice of what was in store for them, with a shot which cannoned off the post. In the 54th minute, a Bluntstone pass found the replacement centre forward and Duff in the Scotland goal was only given a fleeting glimpse of the ball as it flew past him into the back of the net.

Seven minutes later it was 4-0, Hooper providing Duncan with the necessary pass. While twelve minutes later, the Scottish heads fell further as Duncan completed his hat trick with yet another fierce drive that the goalkeeper could do little about. To add to the rout, Haynes added a sixth before the end. Even the partizan Scottish crowd had to applaud what they had just witnessed.

..."I have said before and I repeat it, that Duncan Edwards is certain to be england's future captain"...

In the 'Manchester Evening Chronicle' prior to the local derby match against neighbours City, Alf Clarke wrote..."I have said before and I repeat it, that Duncan Edwards is certain to be england's future captain. Chief problem is where to play him. He is a brilliant wing half back, can also adapt himself to centre half and now both United and England realise his possibilities in attack.

"That is where I think he should be played. That is why United did so well at Huddersfield last weekend and that is why England 'B' won so handsomely at Clyde.

"One international player told me that Edwards might get too heavy. He may be correct in his belief, but I recall that Frank Barson, a former United centre half, was stones too heavy when he returned at the start of a season, but always succeeded in getting down to soccer weight and it never affected his play.

"We cannot escape from the fact that Duncan Edwards is the greatest young player of his age. I know we had our Bastin's, Carter's, Doherty's and others, but I rank Edwards as the best young player I have ever seen".

FEBRUARY 12TH MANCHESTER CITY H 0-5

Duncan retained the number ten jersey as United went out looking for revenge following the F.A. Cup defeat a few weeks previously. Despite his efforts, both in attack and defence, there was no reversal of the result as City lifted their game and recorded a surprising 5-0 victory.

In the newspaper reports that followed, very few United players came through with credit. That is of course with one exception, as Duncan was reported as being here, there and everywhere.

The 'Times' was a classic example, containing the following in a detailed match report - "Manchester United in vivid red, suggested blood and thunder, but with a conspicuous lack of success due mainly to the uncertaincy of Foulkes and Byrne and also their forward line.

"It is not too much to say that the youthful dynamo Edwards, supported in spasms by Gibson and Whitefoot, pretty well faced Manchester City by himself. Understandably, the task was beyond him. But he came close as a touch to creating acute embarrassment to his opponents in an exciting spell before half time."

Good he may have been, but he could not win games on his own.

FEBRUARY 23RD WOLVERHAMPTON WANDERERS H 2-4

Played on a skating rink like surface, Wolves surprised the home support by taking an early lead, but goals from Tommy Taylor and Duncan, within a minute of each other, pulled United back onto level terms, giving the game an added bite.

Somehow, United just couldn't maintain their assault on the Wolves defence and the second half belonged almost entirely to the Midlands side. A further two goals increased their lead and left United struggling as the minutes and the game slipped away from them.

FEBRUARY 26TH CARDIFF CITY A 0-3

Continuing at inside left, Duncan and his United team mates never got going and the home side capitalised on some poor play, both in defence and attack. This defeat made it three in a row, with 12 goals conceded and only two scored.

For once, the ploy of pushing Duncan forward in the hope that his added strength and physical presence would be to United's advantage failed to pay off.

MARCH 5TH BURNLEY H 1-0

United's first League win in a month.

Still playing at inside left and almost opened the scoring in the opening minutes. Johnny Berry worked his way down the right wing and his cross was met perfectly by Duncan who hit the ball without hesitating. McDonald in the Burnley goal stuck up his hands, in hope more than anything else, and was surprised as anyone in the 31,729 crowd when the ball hit them and rebounded over the bar.

An easier chance came his way later in the first half, but from only eight yards out, he shot wide.
Shortly after the second half got underway, a Burnley player, following a tackle with Duncan, complained to the referee about the United man's studs, but an inspection by the referee on the footwear in question resulted in no action being taken.
With sixty-six minutes gone, a Webster shot struck a Burnley player and went for a corner. Scanlon's kick floated into the penalty area and was met firmly by Duncan's head, sending it firmly into the back of the net.
Late in the game only the agility of McDonald prevented him from scoring his and United's second.

A mid-week inter league match provided Duncan with a further opportunity of improving his hopes of a place in the full England line up. Unfortunately, his performance did little to enhance his position in the eyes of the watching selectors, as early in the game he was spoken to by the referee for a needless foul on Gordon Smith and shortly afterwards found himself being booked for another clumsy challenge. This seemed to have an immediate effect in his all round game and dulled his enthusiasm quite a bit.
Four minutes before the interval, with the Football League side winning 1-0, he needlessly handled in the penalty area and from the resulting kick the Scots scored the equaliser. Fortunately, the goal wasn't decisive in any way, as the visitors scored a further two compared to the Scottish League's once.
It was a disappointed Duncan Edwards on the journey home.
Due to the F.A.Cup exit at the hands of Manchester City, Saturday March 12th became blank on the United fixture list. Manager Matt Busby, however, was not generous enough to give his players a rare afternoon off, arranging a friendly at Lincoln to keep his team ticking over. Duncan, was spared the journey, but still had to prepare for a game as the youth team had a fifth round tie against Plymouth Argyle at Old Trafford.
Where to play him was Busby's only problem, with the manager finally deciding to employ his talents in the rather alien centre half spot. Here, he stood like Nelson's column in the middle of Trafalgar Square, except that nothing got round him.
Once again the United lad's proved far too strong for their lesser opponents, scoring nine without reply. Bobby Charlton and Shay Brennan scored three apiece, Beckett , English and Duncan, who bulldozed through the middle to complete the scoring with a ferocious drive. This was two better than their result in the previous round, when Sheffield Wednesday had conceded seven without reply.

MARCH 19TH EVERTON H 1-2

A rather lacklustre display in yet another defeat, the fourth in the last five games.
Once again United failed to do the business in front of their own supporters, as Everton played some fine football and thoroughly deserved their 2-1 win.
United actually took the lead through Scanlon in the 13th minute, but the Goodison park side equalised six minutes before half time, scoring what was to be the winner five minutes after the break.

Perhaps one of the reasons for what was considered a poor performance was the prospect of the England 'B' international against Germany four days later. The last opportunity to make any sort of impression on the England selectors before the forthcoming match against Scotland at the beginning of April.

"Edwards last night was a wing half in the true English tradition. Powerful in everything he did, he was a young colossus"

Never having really suffered from nerves, he had, however, been touted for a full international cap for some time now and with the frustration of United not playing well, perhaps Duncan was trying just that little bit too hard, whilst worrying about his England chances.

Had he read the following days newspaper's, following the 1-1 draw, they would have done little to reassure him regarding his full international call up and left him with mixed feelings. One reporter was quite to the point and wrote - "A rather poor showing and did nothing to claim a place in the full England side to face Scotland in April", while another penned "Edwards last night was a wing half in the true English tradition. Powerful in everything he did, he was a young colossus."

Needless to say, he had a nervous few days to wait until the England side would be announced.

MARCH 26TH PRESTON NORTH END A 2-0

Still performing for United at inside left, but now with Albert Scanlon as a partner, they had established a good understanding. Although the performance, as a team, had improved slightly, Duncan was still far from his best and on one occasion, when he should and would normally have scored, he hurried his shot and missed the target.

As the England squad was due to be named within the next few days, it was obvious that this was still playing on his mind.

Much to his relief and certainly his delight, the name of Duncan Edwards appeared in the England team to face Scotland at Wembley on April 2nd. His selection also brought him the distinction of becoming the youngest player to represent England in a full international, at the age of 18 years and 183 days, since Arthur Brown of Sheffield United (aged 18 years and 10 months) against Wales in February 1904. (It is worth noting that E.C.Bambridge of the Swifts was only 17 when he represented England in 1879).

Not many players can have enjoyed an easier international debut than Duncan (along with Ken Armstrong and Jimmy Meadows), as he had Roger Byrne immediately behind, helping him through the game and his England team mates tore the 'Auld Enemy' apart in a 7-2 humiliation.

Playing in his familiar number six jersey, what he had to do he did well and certainly did not look at all out of place alongside his more illustrious team mates. Wembley was of course, not a new experience and the noise from the packed terraces did little to unnerve him as he enjoyed a pleasurable afternoon.

What then were Duncan's own thoughts on such a memorable occasion? "During the week leading up to the match, I never really gave it much thought. On the Friday, however, I was a little nervous, while on the Saturday not too bad. But by lunchtime on the Saturday, I really had 'butterflies'.

"Once I got to Wembley itself and into the dressing rooms, there were good luck telegrams to read and I began to feel better. All the players wished me luck before we went out and Billy Wright said that if anyone shouted at me just to take it with a pinch of salt".

APRIL 8TH SUNDERLAND A 3-4

It was back to reality and League football six days later with a trip to Sunderland on Good Friday. Still on a high from the previous Saturday and back at inside left, the new international star capped a fine performance with two goals in what was sadly yet another defeat.

Duncan actually gave United the lead after seventeen minutes and he pulled his team level to 3-3 in the 51st minute, only to see the Roker Park side snatch a fourth and both points in what was a disappointing afternoon once again.

APRIL 9TH LEICESTER CITY A 0-1

The visit to Filbert Street once again failed to bring United any rewards for their afternoon's endeavours, but it did earn Duncan a few bruises in what was to become a rather bad tempered affair, with the Leicester players picking him out for some unjust and unnecessary treatment.

APRIL 11TH SUNDERLAND H 2-2

Passed a late fitness test prior to this match and contributed to what could be considered a well earned point, compared with recent results.

This was in fact Duncan's last League match of the season, due to a couple of knocks and the forthcoming F.A. Youth Cup games in the semi-final and possibly the Final.

The United youngsters had scored some 26 goals in the previous five rounds of the competition, but it was widely expected that Chelsea would provide them with a much sterner task than any they had previously encountered this season. The first leg of what promised to be a thrilling semi-final, was played at Stamford Bridge on April 16th, in front of over 20,000 spectators.

With the inclusion of Duncan, the United team took on a look of invincibility, but they were far from being a one-man-team. Captained by the mesmeric Eddie Colman, the line up also contained the likes of Bobby Charlton, Wilf McGuinness and Shay Brennan.

At Stamford Bridge and as it would also unfold in the second leg, it was the full England Internationalist who steered United through to the Final.

"give the ball to the big man at every opportunity".

A goal behind at half time, United had been finding it difficult to break down the Londoners rearguard, but the half time instructions were simple and to the point - "give the ball to the big man at every opportunity".

No sooner had the referee's whistle sounded the start off the second half, than the ball was immediately dispatched to Duncan's feet. Turning quickly, he hit a firm and hard shot which left the Chelsea

goalkeeper helpless as it flew past him into the net. The game suddenly took on a completely different shape as Chelsea soon found themselves more and more on the defensive, as United pushed forward for the winner.

Within ten minutes, they were indeed in front. The goal scorer? Duncan Edwards.

Gathering the ball in a position of little danger to Chelsea's, some forty yards out, he lumbered forward, brushing aside any attempted challenges. Lifting his head slightly, while still twenty-five yards from goal, he steadied himself before launching the ball once again goal wards. 2-1 to United and that was indeed that.

In the second leg two days later on April 18th, Chelsea, with hopes of turning the 2-1 deficit around, travelled north to Manchester. Once again they performed valiantly, but as in the previous meeting, the

"He is, as they say, football daft".

score line and the semi-final was determined by one player. The scoreline once again read 2-1 in United's favour, with the scorer of both goals - Duncan Edwards.

The appearance of Duncan in both legs of the semi-final and of course scoring all four United goals had not gone unnoticed and in some quarters did not go down too well, due to the fact that he was a United regular and now an England international.

Indeed, such was the ill feeling surrounding his inclusion in the United Youth team that Matt Busby dedicated most of his Manchester Evening Chronicle article in the 'Saturday Pink' of April 23rd to the subject.

He wrote "A London friend told me that Manchester United were "not playing fair" in their Youth cup competition progress by including Duncan Edwards the 18 year old international.

" 'Oh yes' he said,'I know that he qualifies by age, but here is a player who has actually played for England at Wembley, is included in the England touring party going to France, Italy and Portugal in the close season and has also secured other representative honours'.

"He then added, 'I was addressing a meeting of soccer referee's the other night and the question cropped up. The general opinion was that Manchester United should not include him in their Youth team'.

"So that's what some people think. It annoys me! Duncan is eligible to participate in the Youth Cup. And, what is more, is keen to play. He is no seeker of cup's and medal's, but he is just as anxious as any other United young player to have the United name inscribed on the Cup for the third successive season. It would be an achievement which, perhaps may never be equalled.

"He may be 'outsize' in juniors, but he will probably tell you that he has to work just as hard - if not harder- in the Youth Cup competition as in senior football.

"He is, as they say, 'football daft'. He dreams football and loves to talk about it and is eager to learn everything he can from the game. Duncan Edwards has not become a great footballer by bulldozer tactics. He is undoubtedly one of the greatest examples we have ever had of a footballer maturing at an early age.

"But if the rules of the competition mean that he is eligible to take part, then I see no earthly reason to quibble, I don't doubt that if other club's had the opportunity they would willingly include him in their Youth side.

"Duncan Edwards has come to the front the hard way. That is by constant training and coaching. The United youngster never needs to be told what to do - though he is not alone in that respect.

"He, like others, is determined to make a success of his career as a footballer. He is willing to listen to

..."Here is an 18 year old whose example can be a lesson to every soccer-thinking youth"...

advice and put that advice into practise on the field. Here is an 18 year old whose example can be a lesson to every soccer-thinking youth.

"I am happy to think that Duncan is getting so many honours from the game. I am glad to know that he remains as keen a player in junior soccer circles as in representative games.

"But to suggest that because of his exceptional talent he should not play in Youth games is in my opinion ridiculous."

United's opponents in the Final of the F.A. Youth Cup were West Bromwich Albion, with the first leg at Old Trafford on April 27th . In front of over 16,000 spectators, United showed the Midland lads little compassion and goals from Colman 2, Beckett and Charlton, against a solitary reply from the visitors left United with more than one hand on the trophy.

At the Hawthorns three days later, United again took command, increasing their lead through Charlton, before Duncan scored his last F.A. Youth cup goal to make it 6-1 on aggregate. A late own goal made it 3-0 on the night and 7-1 on aggregate.

At the final whistle, a cheer went up from the United team, officials and supporters, while a larger sigh of relief was more audible around the country, with the knowledge that Duncan Edwards had played his last match at this level.

Much to everyone's despair, however, even without Duncan Edwards in the team, the United youths were still unstoppable, winning the competition again in the following two seasons.

CHAPTER FIVE
UNITED, ENGLAND, THE ARMY AND THE CHAMPIONSHIP

The close season of 1955 was shorter than normal for Duncan Edwards, as in common with almost all other teenage males, he was called up to do his two years National Service in June. He accepted it as a minor inconvenience to his footballing career and typically shrugged his shoulders and got on with it. The training kept him physically fit, he had other footballers for company, with the only minus point being the travelling now involved in playing for United. Instead of jumping on a Manchester Corporation bus for Old Trafford, he had to travel back from his Shrewsbury base in order to meet up with his team mates.

AUGUST 20TH BIRMINGHAM CITY A 2-2

Birmingham City missed a few chances before Dennis Viollet gave United the lead, but United's play was soon hampered by a thigh injury to Tommy Taylor, forcing him to play wide on the wing as a virtual passenger. This provided the visitors with the opportunity to get back into the game, one that they gratefully accepted and the quickly drew level.
Viollet, with a second goal, once again put United in front, but to their credit, Birmingham kept plodding away and with only six minutes to play, once again scored an equaliser and held on for the remaining minutes to earn a point.

AUGUST 24TH TOTTENHAM HOTSPUR H 2-2

Once again, United had to be content with a share of the points in a closely fought match with Tottenham. Goals from outside right Johnny Berry and Colin Webster, deputising for the injured Tommy Taylor, were United's goalscorers.

AUGUST 27TH WEST BROMWICH ALBION H 3-1

After something of an ordinary start to his season, Duncan began to show much of the form that had brought him success in the earlier half of the year. Following two drawn games, United also found their winning ways again and the commanding display by Duncan went a long way to ensuring both points.
In the 48th minute, he made the second goal. Winning possession on the halfway line, he ran a few yards with the ball before slipping it inside to Dennis Viollett to score.
With one United attack, it looked as if a scoring opportunity had fell to Duncan, but his effort not only missed the intended target, but disappeared out of the ground!

AUGUST 31ST TOTTENHAM HOTSPUR A 2-1

If his shooting was a little off target against West Bromwich Albion, he certainly made up for it against Tottenham, with both goals in United's 2-1 win.

The first goal came after only three minutes, with Duncan pouncing on a lose ball following a corner and with a combination of strength and skill forced his way through a collection of bodies, before hitting an unstoppable left footed shot from just outside the penalty box, low into the Tottenham net.

His second, in the 41st minute came via a pass from Eddie Lewis and once again from just outside the area he unleashed a powerful shot that flew into the far corner.

The acceptance and ease with which Duncan executed both goals once again opened the debate as to his best position. It was purely because of his performance that United defeated Tottenham, with his fine sense of positioning and strength while on the ball adding much to United's game as a whole.

SEPTEMBER 3RD MANCHESTER CITY A 0-1

An injury to Dennis Viollett saw Duncan wearing the number ten jersey in the first 'derby' match of the season at Maine road. It was to be a disappointing day all round though as the home side came out on top in a rather disappointing and dour ninety minutes with little going right for the individual or the team.

The switch to the forward line had not paid off and it was suggested that he did not posses the finesse of Viollett, nor was he a schemer or a player who could latch onto the half chance to create a goal out of nothing.

SEPTEMBER 7TH EVERTON H 2-1

Duncan was again at inside left, in what was considered a scrappy struggle. One reporter of the time commented that "United won because of their youthful fervour, expressed so well in the runaway bus dashes of inside forward Duncan Edwards".

With the visitors 1-0 in front, Duncan was involved in a controversial equaliser in the 60th minute. Heading a lobbed clearance by Everton centre half Jones against the underside of the bar, this created a scramble which resulted in O'Neill in the Everton goal pushing the ball away. Much to the surprise of the visitors and the delight of Duncan, the referee awarded the goal, but the Everton players fiercely debated it. Their captain, Peter Farrell was later to say "it was never a goal, as it did not cross the line".

"United won because of their youthful fervour, expressed so well in the runaway bus dashes of inside forward Duncan Edwards"

The match against Everton, was to be the last Duncan would play until mid-October, as he missed United's next seven fixtures due to influenza, which saw him admitted to Davyhulme Pak Hospital and kept under observation.

It wasn't long before he was on his feet again and out and about. One Sunday afternoon a decision to go for a cup of coffee with a friend, while passing the time at Manchester's Ringway Airport, brought a complete change to his life. While enjoying the leisurely afternoon, he was introduced to 20 year old Molly Leach and they immediately hit it off.

"...he has been accepted as United's regular left half and as such has won England's white"

They were to meet as regular as possible after that with visits to the cinema and the theatre becoming commonplace if they decided to go out, but they were quite happy to stay in and listen to records or play cards. Duncan had never been one for nightclubs, so they seldom went dancing. "He only did the slow ones" declared Molly.

His love life, however, did produce an unwanted and embarrassing brush with the law. One night, while cycling back to his digs from Molly's, a policeman stopped him, as he had no lights on his bicycle. This 'crime' resulted in no simple rebuke from the constable, but an appearance before Sale Magistrates, resulting in a 10/- (50p) fine.

During Duncan's enforced absence, United had a mixed bag of results, winning three, losing two and drawing the other two of the seven games. His all-round ability was sorely missed and needless to say he missed his football.

He returned to the United side on October 19th for a friendly in Glasgow against Clyde and his re-appearance in the team was not only something that his colleagues were looking forward to, but the 'Daily Record' columnist 'Waverley' was also keen to see him in action again. In his column on the day of the match he wrote - "One of the men I want to see again in the United team is wing half Edwards. This teenager got his big chance at Kilmarnock a couple of years back when Cockburn was injured and Edwards, not yet 17, came on as substitute.

"Since then he has been accepted as United's regular left half and as such has won England's white."

Sadly his return to the fold did not inspire United and once again, Clyde recorded a victory against their notable opponents. They followed up their 4-1 win last season with a 2-1 win this time around.

OCTOBER 22ND HUDDERSFIED TOWN H 3-0

Considering the length of time he had been out of action and his inability to train, Duncan turned in a commendable performance. He enthusiastically got involved in everything and at one point a little too much so, as the referee had to speak to him following a foul on Cavanagh. He had certainly not lost any of his shooting power, as one attempt came close, with Huddersfield's goalkeeper Wheeler having to scurry across his goal to turn the ball round the post.

OCTOBER 29TH CARDIFF CITY A 1-0

As United fought against a spirited Cardiff side, it was Duncan Edwards who came closest to breaking the deadlock with a couple of fine efforts which went narrowly wide of the post.
Cardiff's right sided players were certainly finding the going tough against the United wing half.
In the end, a solitary Tommy Taylor goal was all that separated the two sides.

United's 1-0 win over Cardiff at Ninian Park, saw them move to the top of the First Division, with Duncan now looking as sharp as ever. So much so, that he found himself selected to represent the British Army XI for the first time, with a place in the team to face Rangers at Ibrox on November 2nd.
Colonel Mitchell, who was in charge of the Army side, said that he was playing Duncan at centre forward "to strengthen the attack". This promised to provide Duncan with something of a test, as he was up against the highly experienced Scotland centre-half George Young. When asked for his thoughts about playing against such an accomplished professional, Duncan replied simply, "I hope we both have a good game".
As it worked out, the Rangers cornerstone enjoyed the best of the ninety minutes, with the correspondent for the Glasgow Herald who attended the match writing - "The young centre-forward had an extremely poor night against George Young. Indeed, when the game was only ten minutes old, he seemed to realise that he had scant chance of doing anything in the centre of the field. From then on, he roved both right and left wings, leaving Young complete control in defence".
This was no more than a one-off, as five days later, he was turning in a "notable performance", in a 2-2 draw, alongside team mates Bill Foulkes, Eddie Colman and Tommy Taylor against a FA XI at Newcastle in front of 5,700 spectators.

NOVEMBER 5TH ARSENAL H 1-1

With an international match against Spain on the near horizon, the watching England selectors left Old Trafford much relieved by the performance of the United wing half, who was by far the best player on the pitch. This was clearly the Duncan Edwards of old with his energy sapping bout of influenza and poor performance for the Army side in Glasgow put clearly behind him.

NOVEMBER 12TH BOLTON WANDERERS A 1-3

United debutant Eddie Colman was the wing half in the news, not his more illustrious partner.
United started this game well, with a goal from Tommy Taylor after only three minutes, but soon faded, allowing the home side to gain the advantage and by the interval they were 2-1 in front.
The second half saw United remain on the defensive, with little in the way of scoring opportunities, although they did succeed in keeping Bolton at bay. With the game in its final minute, the home side eventually scored a third. United's first defeat in nine games.

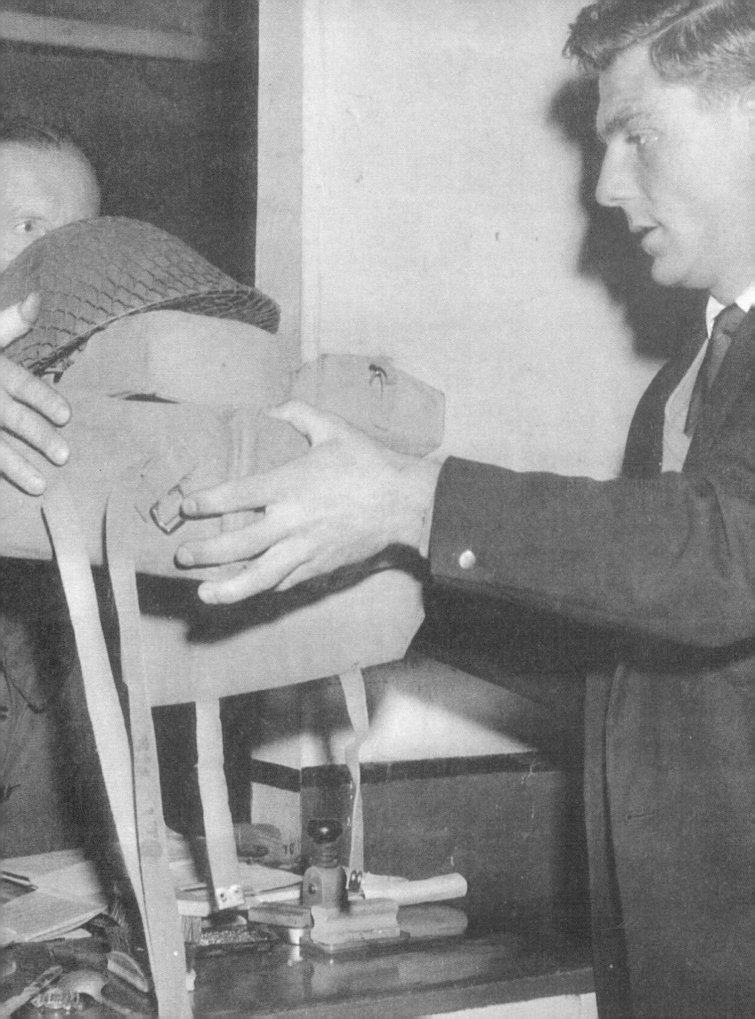

NOVEMBER 19TH CHELSEA H 3-0

Victory against the current League Champions maintained United's position at the top of the First Division and increased their unbeaten post-war run against London sides to 38 games.

Despite the convincing score-line, it was at times something of a physical encounter between the two sides. At one point, with Duncan forcing his way through the Chelsea defence, he was caught on the ankle by Armstrong and much to his annoyance, his appeal for a free-kick was turned down by the referee. As the official waved play on, Duncan, surprisingly out of character, angrily turned on Armstrong, giving him a piece of his mind, only to be spoken to by the referee for the confrontation.

NOVEMBER 26TH BLACKPOOL A 0-0

"Edwards was working like a Trojan and he beat man after man..."

Duncan was soon in the thick of things and Alf Clarke in the Manchester Evening News wrote - "Edwards was working like a Trojan and he beat man after man, trying to force his way through, only to be upended 25 yards from goal." The resulting free kick was taken by Byrne, with a short pass to Duncan, but his goal bound shot was deflected for a corner.

Duncan, more than anyone, was trying to make the necessary breakthrough against a strong Blackpool defence, but to no avail, as United's Championship challengers held on for a hard earned point.

DECEMBER 3RD SUNDERLAND H 2-1

Three weeks previously, against Bolton Wanderers at Burnden Park, one of Duncan's best friends, Eddie Colman made his United debut and against Sunderland they showed that they were more than capable of forming an exciting wing half partnership for United and possibly in the future for England. It was the much bigger of the two individuals who stole the show with a commanding display

At one point, it looked as though he was in trouble after having received a knock and might have to leave the field, but he carried on regardless and finished the match as strong as ever.

DECEMBER 10TH PORTSMOUTH A 2-3

For the second Saturday running, the opposition's tackling left a bit to be desired and Duncan was again on the receiving end. Such tactics failed to make any impression on the player, other than make him want to try that little bit harder and minutes after pulling up following one challenge he came close to getting his revenge when his shot flew narrowly past the Portsmouth post.

Although his inspirational play created numerous opportunities for his forwards, he could do little about the outcome of the match, which United lost by the odd goal in five. He was, however, the centre of attention as the opposing number six, Jimmy Dickinson, was his main challenger for the England left half position.

The ball was clearly in Duncan's court to show that he was the best left half in the country, as Dickinson had failed to impress in the recent International against Spain and the Inter-League meeting against the League of Ireland. Since his return from illness, Duncan on the other hand had continued to show the level of consistency in his play that was one of his main attributes.

At the end of the ninety minutes, it was the visitor from Manchester who came out on top, even although his team failed in the battle for the points, (they lead 1-0 at half time and conceded two goals in the last five minutes), turning in yet another notable performance, breaking up Portsmouth attacks and setting his own forwards in motion. There was only one man who the England selectors could consider for forthcoming Internationals.

DECEMBER 17TH BIRMINGHAM CITY H 2-1

United maintained their unbeaten record, with a promising display defensively in the second half, but at times were inclined to make hard work of things.

Duncan was prominent in United's defence as Birmingham City tried to claw their way back into the game, but the rearguard stood firm.

DECEMBER 24TH WEST BROMWICH ALBION A 4-1

A dazzling first half display was United's best of the season, with the home side totally bewildered.

DECEMBER 26TH CHARLTON ATHLETIC H 5-1
DECEMBER 27TH CHARLTON ATHLETIC A 0-3

Two completely contrasting results against Charlton, with United complete overwhelming their London opponents in a 5-1 Boxing Day mauling. Twenty-four hours later it was an entirely different story at the Valley with Charlton gaining revenge, scoring thrice without reply.

DECEMBER 31ST MANCHESTER CITY H 2-1

A post war record crowd of 60,956 packed Old Trafford for the first 'derby' of the season and the majority of them enjoyed the United victory. Perhaps it was the tension and the knife edge atmosphere of the clash between the local rivals, but it produced a rare lapse in concentration and show of dissent from Duncan.

Trying to be a little too clever, when challenged by Spurdle, he conceded a corner kick. For one reason or another, he disapproved of the referee's decision and flung the ball over the touchline in a petulant gesture, which needless to say brought him an instant rebuke from the official.

The first fixture of the New Year was the third round F.A. Cup tie against Bristol Rovers, which produced something of a major shock, to say the least. Losing 4-0, United just did not perform on the day. Perhaps the presence of Duncan in the side made more of a difference than people though, or anyone cared to mention, as he was a notable absentee from the cup tie line up with a septic knee. Needless to say, he was sorely missed.

JANUARY 14TH SHEFFIELD UNITED H 3-1

Returning to the United side, Duncan showed no ill effects from the septic knee which had caused problems over the last couple of weeks. Once again his link-up play with wing half partner Eddie Colman was widely commented on and praised, as was his all round performance. Back to his best.

JANUARY 21ST PRESTON NORTH END A 1-3

No luck for United as Preston won their first game at home against the Championship challengers for some time.
United fielded something of a weakened side, with Scott and Webster replacing Berry and Taylor depriving the forward line from some of its punch. It was rather surprising that manager Matt Busby did not consider it worth while moving Duncan forward to strengthen the attack.

Not having scored since September, Duncan was more than pleased to get back on the goal trail, even although it was just in a friendly match against Leeds United at Elland Road, United winning 4-1, organised due to the F.A.Cup dismissal at the hands of Bristol Rovers earlier in the month. It was a match Duncan should actually have missed, as he had been selected for the Army side to face Dundee, but due to bad weather, this fixture was postponed.
Life in the Army was considered "not too bad", perhaps only because it provided the opportunity of playing more football and it was not uncommon for Duncan to be playing two, sometimes three games per week. Since his debut in the Army side at Ibrox, back in October, he had featured regularly in the team and his performances at this level were little different than those in the Football League while wearing the red of United and 'man of the match' acclaim was just as regular.
One such performance was, funnily enough, in Scotland against East Fife on January 30th. Perhaps he felt that he had something to prove to the Scottish footballing public following his poor showing against Rangers and in-different perfomance against Clyde.
The Army, despite their talented team of individuals, found themselves 1-0 down at half time and a re-shuffle at the interval saw Duncan move forward from his left half position of the first forty five minutes

to inside left, in the hope of producing something from the game.

Not one to disappoint although he had missed a good scoring opportunity early on when right through with only the goalkeeper to beat, Duncan, forming a fine partnership with Omond of Queens Park, turned the game around with the 1-0 scoreline changing to 2-1 in the Army's favour.

Making amends for his earlier miss, Duncan scored the equaliser in the 59th minute, walking a pass from the aforementioned Omond into the East Fife net.

Duncan, despite his muscular build, strength in the tackle and powerful shooting, never used his attributes unfairly, however, during the latter stages of this match one unfortunate individual was to feel the effects of coming into contact with the United powerhouse.

With fifteen minutes remaining, Duncan connected with the ball in front of the home goal. Steedman, the East Fife goalkeeper, could do little to get out of the way and knew nothing about the point blank shot as the ball caught him full on the face, knocking him unconscious. The unfortunate custodian was carried from the field suffering from concussion and the home side saw out the game with only ten men.

FEBRUARY 4TH BURNLEY H 2-0

Back on the winning trail, with goals from Taylor and Viollet, in a match played in poor conditions on a slippery surface. This extended the unbeaten run to 15 games.

Having played for the England under 23 side against their Scottish counterparts at Hillsborough Sheffield on February 8th, Duncan's hectic life style continued, with selection for the British Army against the Belgian Army in Brussels, in a competition known as the 'Kentish Cup', three days later. Unfortunately for United manager Matt Busby, Bill Foulkes and Eddie Colman were also called upon for this fixture, forcing him into making unwanted changes for the match against Luton Town due to be played the previous day.

The journey to the Belgian capital was made by coach to the south coast and then across the English Channel by ferry. Unfortunately for the footballing soldiers, the crossing was made in poor conditions with the boat lurching about on the choppy seas. Most of the team coped well enough with the unwelcome conditions, but Duncan, who didn't care much for flying added ferries to his list of pet hates, as he lay in a cabin being violently sick as the boat pitched up and down as it cut its way through the water.

By the time the party reached dry land, he certainly did not feel like ninety minutes of football and much to his relief and possibly that of some of his team-mates they discovered that the fixture had been postponed due to bad weather. Fortunately for Duncan, the return crossing was much smoother.

FEBRUARY 18TH WOLVERHAMPTON WANDERERS A 2-0

A good two points on a snow covered Molineux, with the defensive trio of Byrne, Jones and Edwards (back in the side following Army duty last week) well in command. A good result considering that

United's last three fixtures played on this ground had been lost.
With United a goal in front, Duncan was to his surprise penalised for hand ball. Much to his relief, Hancocks blazed his kick well over.

FEBRUARY 25TH ASTON VILLA H 1-0

Another match played out on a snow covered pitch, which was hard underneath.
Whelan's second half goal gave United both points and kept up the momentum in the Championship chase.
United sat on top of the table with 44 points from 38 games, with Blackpool second, six points behind.

MARCH 3RD CHELSEA A 4-2

Chelsea scored two goals inside a minute to take a surprise lead, but Pegg pulled one back in the 27th minute to keep United in the game. Just before the interval, Duncan almost scored the equaliser, but his shot was deflected wide for a corner.
After the interval, it was all United and goals from Taylor and a Dennis Viollet double saw United take both points.

MARCH 10TH CARDIFF CITY H 1-1

"After stopping a Cardiff attack, he went racing through on goal..."

It was almost two years and eleven months to the day that Duncan Edwards had made his United League debut against Cardiff City and during that time he had matured into one of the finest players in the country. In something of an anniversary celebration, he once again demonstrated to the public his prolific footballing skills.
"A magnificent game" proclaimed one newspaper report. "After stopping a Cardiff attack, he went racing through on goal to put a 40 yard drive just wide of the post". It continued, "His tackle prevented a corner and his long clearance downfield to the unmarked Viollett, saw the United forward fouled in the box, with Byrne scoring from the resulting penalty".

MARCH 17TH ARSENAL A 1-1

A dropped point at Highbury, on a day when Blackpool beat Newcastle United 5-1 to close the gap at the top to five points with a game in hand.

Byrne missed a penalty which did not help and following Arsenal's equaliser in the 76th minute, tempers became frayed as United fought to hang on for the point.

MARCH 24TH BOLTON WANDERERS H 1-0

Two hard earned points in a gripping Lancashire 'derby', brought the title a little closer.

The United defence was well on top, with Duncan keeping Nat Lofthouse well under control. A Tommy Taylor goal was enough to win the game.

MARCH 30TH NEWCASTLE UNITED H 5-2

With the title firmly in their sights, United totally demoralised their North West visitors with a five star performance, with all the forwards bar Johnny Berry getting on the score sheet.

The first half could have gone either way, but the second forty five minutes saw the game burst into life with four goals in twenty nine minutes, three of them coming in a furious nine minutes.

A Duncan Edwards blunder had let Newcastle steal an equaliser to make it 1-1, but at the end of the day, it mattered little.

MARCH 31ST HUDDERSFIELD TOWN A 2-0

Tommy Taylor's 99th and 100th League goals gave United both points against a Huddersfield side fighting for their lives at the foot of the table, level on points with Villa.

United were now seven points clear with Blackpool still having a game in hand.

APRIL 2ND NEWCASTLE UNITED A 0-0

The tension in the race for the Championship was beginning to show, as having beaten Newcastle 5-2 four days previously, when Duncan gifted the visitors a goal which levelled the score at 1-1, United found the going tough at St James Park.

Duncan was forced to work hard in order to stem the Newcastle attacks, whilst also finding time to join in the attack, on one occasion coming close to breaking the deadlock, with Simpson saving just under the bar. At the end of the ninety minutes, United had to be grateful for the point, with the forthcoming visit of Blackpool to Old Trafford the confrontation that would decide the outcome of the Championship trophy.

APRIL 7TH BLACKPOOL H 2-1

Needless to say, Old Trafford was packed to the rafters and the gates shut well before kick-off, 62,277 inside and thousands more still outside as the two Lancashire rivals prepared for the vital ninety minutes.

After only ninety seconds, an eerie silence enveloped the ground when Durie put the visitors ahead and they remained so for the remainder of the first half as United tired in vain to claw their way back into the game.

A head injury to Tommy Taylor did little to help the cause, but with the centre forward off the field receiving treatment, a desperate lunge at Doherty by Farm in the Blackpool goal brought United a penalty. Up stepped Johnny Berry. 1-1.

It was all United now, with Duncan seeming to cover every blade of grass on the Old Trafford turf. One minute he was the corner stone of the defence, the next up alongside his forwards looking for the goal which could decide the match and indeed the Championship itself.

The minutes ticked away and it was beginning to look as if the title was not going to be decided there and then. Blackpool were as desperate in their search for the illusive goal as their hosts, but with only ten minutes remaining, Berry, not for the first time in the match, skipped his way down the touch-line past the bemused Blackpool full-back. His cross, found the patched up Taylor a yard or so from goal, who prodded the ball goal-wards. Firth on the goal line made a drastic, valiant attempt to stop the ball with his hand and prevent it from crossing the line.

For a second, Old Trafford was silent. Suddenly, the referee turned, pointed up-field, he had given the goal. United were in front. The crowd erupted. Minutes later, a greater sound of relief and acclaim emitted from their throats, United were Champions.

Duncan once again found himself journeying north over Hadrians Wall to battle with the Scots, this time at Hampden against the national side, one week after savouring his first Championship success. The

"...Early in the second half he upended one of the Scottish forwards, Legget I think it was, and every time he got the ball or went near one of the Scottish players after that, he was heartily booed by sections of the crowd"

sound, which greeted Duncan as he emerged from the dressing rooms with his England team was much different and certainly louder than that which had greeted the final whistle at Old Trafford seven days earlier, but it was one that Duncan was determined to silence.

"I had seen Duncan play quite a few times" recalled Bob Forsyth, a 24 year old squashed alongside many others on the vast terraces of the Glasgow ground that afternoon. " I had actually seen him come on as substitute at Kilmarnock as something of a raw youngster a couple of years previously and had followed his career from a distance ever since. Watching him against Scotland that afternoon, you could notice how much he had developed, both physically and as a player in such a short time.

"He almost scored, I remember, when Hewie misjudged a clearance. His first time effort went narrowly wide. In one way, I was grateful, as I would probably shouted my appreciation, which may not have gone down too well. Early in the second half he upended one of the Scottish forwards, Legget I think it was, and every time he got the ball or went near one of the Scottish players after that, he was heartily booed by sections of the crowd."

With only a minute or so remaining, Duncan combined with Johnny Haynes and the ball was crossed towards Tommy Taylor. The United forward headed the ball back into the path of Haynes, who chested it down before scoring.

APRIL 21ST PORTSMOUTH H 1-0

In a game that mattered little result wise, the crowd were treated to a rather half hearted encounter with the solitary goal scored after only nineteen minutes.

With still two minutes of the game to play, the referee blew for a free kick and thinking it was the full time whistle, part of the crowd invaded the pitch. They were eventually cleared, but repeated the invasion when the referee did indeed signal the end of the match.

Manchester United's domestic season came to an end with the presentation of the League Championship trophy, but there was to be no immediate period of relaxation, looking back on a memorable season, as the United directors had arranged a four match tour of Denmark in early May. Due to international commitments, Duncan flew with his United team mates to Gothenburg, played in the opening match of the tour, then returned to England in order to meet up with the England party as they prepared for four games, one at home and three abroad.

Wednesday May 9th, saw the multi-talented Brazilian international side visit Wembley, which produced a highly entertaining ninety minutes for the 97,000 spectators.

The England half back line of Ronnie Clayton, Billy Wright and Duncan were the backbone of the home side, but were disappointed to see a 2-0, five minute lead, pegged back to 2-2 shortly after the interval. Despite numerous missed chances, England over-came the ball playing South American's and two late goals saw the intriguing ninety minutes end 4-2 in England's favour.

With a three match continental tour arranged by the Football Association, there was little time for Duncan to enjoy much of a rest before packing his bags and setting off for Sweden, the first stop on the itinerary.

A disappointing performance in the Rasunda Stadium on May 16th, ended in a goal less draw, while four days later Finland were convincingly defeated 5-1. It was, however, the final match of the mini-tour that produced the best performance by both the team and Duncan.

Against World Champions West Germany, in a packed Berlin Olympic Stadium, the crowd were treated to a memorable display and took the imposing figure of Duncan Edwards into their hearts, even although he was on the opposition side.

"...the German media quickly christened him "Boom Boom Edwards", much to his embarrassment..."

With 25 minutes gone, Duncan was picked out with a throw from Reg Matthews in the England goal. Still inside his own half, Duncan set off in familiar fashion towards the German goal. Surprisingly and to their obvious ignorance, the German's allowed him to move forward with the ball. A couple of innocuous challenges were easily avoided and from a couple of steps inside the penalty area the ball was propelled past the helpless goalkeeper into the back of the net. The crowd, with a sprinkling of British servicemen among the 100,000, rose as one to acclaim an excellent goal, his first in an England jersey. Such was the power of Duncan's shot, the German media quickly christened him "Boom Boom Edwards", much to his embarrassment and the mickey taking of his England team-mates. Yet again, Duncan Edwards had extended his now world wide fan club.

CHAPTER SIX
THE EUROPEAN ADVENTURE

Having won the League Championship, Manchester United received an invitation to take part in the European Cup, a competition in its second season, which brought together the Champions from various European countries in a home and away knock out tournament. Manager Matt Busby was enthusiastic to say the least, about this new innovation, as he felt that there was much to be gained by facing the top continental sides. He convinced his board to accept the invitation, but found opposition in the Football League Management Committee, although an ally in the Football Association.

Eventually the Football League backed down, United were in the European Cup and Duncan Edwards would have even more travelling to do in what was to turn out an action packed season.

AUGUST 18TH BIRMINGHAM CITY H 2-2

Despite being played in extremely wet conditions, it was a clean, hard game.

Merrick in the Birmingham goal kept United at bay, with fine saves from Duncan and Tommy Taylor and when Birmingham went 2-1 in front it looked as if United were going to begin the defence of their title with a defeat.

Duncan, however, had other thoughts and "combining the power of a battleship with the manoeuvrability of a destroyer", he rekindled the attack and inspired United to an equaliser with only nine minutes to go.

AUGUST 20TH PRESTON NORTH END A 3-1

Preston had no answer to a powerful United performance, with Tommy Taylor scoring twice and Billy Whelan adding a third.

The half back line of Eddie Colman, Mark Jones and Duncan were always in command and the Preston forwards seldom troubled their visitors.

AUGUST 25TH WEST BROMWICH ALBION A 3-2

Continuing his fine start to the season, Duncan turned in a prominent display against the Midlands side, keeping their persistent attack well under control.

AUGUST 29TH PRESTON NORTH END H 3-2

A much more spirited performance by Preston than that of nine days previously, but once again they had no real answer to the direct play of United, or to be more exact, that of hat trick hero Dennis Viollet.

SEPTEMBER 1ST PORTSMOUTH H 3-0

For the fifth game in a row, United scored three goals and like their previous opponents, Portsmouth could offer little resistance.
Billy Whelan took the plaudits with a superb performance, playing a major part in all three goals. Once again, the United half back line controlled the game from start to finish.

SEPTEMBER 5TH CHELSEA A 2-1

"...Edwards is a giant both in thrusting attack after attack and in covering Byrne in any emergencies"

Following an excellent performance at Stamford Bridge, comparisons were being made between the present side and that of 1948, with the current defence considered much better. "This is especially true at half back" declared the Times football correspondent, "where Edwards is a giant both in thrusting attack after attack and in covering Byrne in any emergencies."

SEPTEMBER 8TH NEWCASTLE UNITED A 1-1

Just before the interval, the referee spoke him to for unceremoniously upending Jackie Milburn, but he was completely unperturbed and almost immediately opened the scoring. Pegg's cross was turned back by Berry and Duncan hit the ball first time only to see his shot hit the foot of the post and then be scrambled away.
As the game went on, he was more prominent in defence than attack, thwarting the Newcastle forwards time and again, depriving both Milburn and Davies of good scoring opportunities.

SEPTEMBER 15TH SHEFFIELD WEDNESDAY H 4-1

"Quixall Held Fast in Edwards Grip" proclaimed one of the many headlines following this Lancashire/Yorkshire war of the roses. The latest 'Golden Boy' of English football, Albert Quixall, was snuffed out of the game by the tigerish tackling of Duncan and throughout the ninety minutes was rarely given room to breathe let alone manoeuvre with the ball.

It was rare to see Duncan employed in a man to man marking job, but he did so with his usual capable assurance and still found the odd opportunity to get involved in other areas of the game.

SEPTEMBER 22ND MANCHESTER CITY H 2-0

United maintained their top of the table position with a convincing 2-0 win over neighbours City, in what was Duncan's 100th Football League appearance for the club. A notable milestone and one which could have been passed last season had it not been for injury, Youth team or Army XI call ups.

"there was not a better pair of wing halves in the country than Edwards and Colman"

The complements directed towards the United wing half pairing of Duncan and his team mate and off field friend Eddie Colman were becoming more regular, with City's Don Revie the latest to join their 'fan club'. Following the match, he said "there was not a better pair of wing halves in the country than Edwards and Colman."

In the 'Times', their correspondent wrote - " Edwards is truly a young giant. He covered all the fir" in defence, dominating everyone in the air. Some thirty yard passes whistled out to Pegg and once with a prodigious nod he turned the ball back to Wood from outside the penalty area. Yet for all his size he can stroke the most delicate pass even when going at full tilt."

SEPTEMBER 26TH ANDERLECHT H 10-0 EUROPEAN CUP   Pr. R 2nd leg

Having missed United's initial appearance in the European Cup with a toe injury, Duncan was eager to get into competitive action against European opposition. Already 2-0 up from the first leg in Brussels, United were keen to maintain their advantage and despite having to play their home games at Maine Road, due to the Old Trafford ground having no floodlights. They turned in a performance, which many at home knew that they were capable of, but at the same time, alerted Europe to the quality of the English Champions.

At the end of the ninety minutes, the Belgians were devastated, having been overwhelmed in an outstanding display of attacking football which would have beaten any team from home or abroad. The night belonged to the United forward line with goals from Viollett 4, Taylor 3, Whelan 2 and Berry, with the only member of the front line not to score, David Pegg, involved in most. Duncan for once was out shadowed.

For the players of today, the twenty-four hours after a mid-week game are spent relaxing and resting the tired limbs. They would be shocked therefore to learn that the day after having been a member of the United side who defeated Anderlecht, he was playing for the Army in a cup-tie.

SEPTEMBER 29TH ARSENAL A 2-1

"...Edwards the courageous, doing two men's work..."

The 'Manchester Evening Chronicle' United correspondent Alf Clarke was quick to pick up on the frequency of which Duncan was now playing, writing in his match report... "Edwards the courageous, doing two men's work. You would not think that this was his fourth game in a week, judging by his brilliance today."

International duty prevented Duncan from playing against Charlton Athletic at Old Trafford and while a youngster called Bobby Charlton was making his mark with a couple of goals on his United debut, Duncan was entertaining the people of Northern Ireland to a rare glimpse of his many talents in a 1-1 draw. Unfortunately the England performance as a whole was rather disappointing and in some quarters, the Irish inside forward, Jimmy McIlroy of Burnley, was given credit for his performance against Duncan.

OCTOBER 13TH SUNDERLAND A 3-1

Viollet scored his 11th goal of the season to give United the lead, but was considered lucky not to be given offside. Sunderland, to their credit, quickly fought back and were soon on level terms, but from then on, it was all United.
Four minutes after the interval, Whelan made it 2-1 and an own goal put the result beyond doubt, with 17 minutes still to play as United continued their unbeaten start to the season.

OCTOBER 17TH BORUSSIA DORTMUND H 3-2 EUROPEAN CUP 1ST Rnd. 1ST Leg

Duncan's performances were not always reported in the nations sports pages with glowing appraisals and complements and in his summary of the game for the 'News Chronicle - Daily Dispatch', Frank Taylor criticised the performance of both Manchester United as a team and Duncan as an individual.

He wrote that United appeared to be a little too cocky, perhaps something to do with their previous display against Anderlecht and were fortunate not to actually lose to the Germans. Duncan and his sidekick Eddie Colman received a written reprimand for not getting a grip of the game and using their skills to United's advantage.

OCTOBER 20TH EVERTON H 2-5

Following the criticism in the press regarding his performance in the mid week European Cup tie, the visit of Everton to Old Trafford brought even more despair for the United number six.
An injury in the first half, forced him to leave the field for treatment and upon returning he struggled to maintain anything like his normal form. With a minute to play before half time, and Everton already 2-1 in front, he presented the visitors with the opportunity to go further ahead.
With all the time in the world to clear the ball, as he stood just inside the centre circle, he hesitated for one reason or another and was promptly robbed of the ball by Gauld. A quick through ball from the Everton player to his team mate Eglington caught the United defence flat footed and the visitors were 3-1 in front.
The second forty-five minutes saw the individual and his team fare little better as Everton scored a further two goals, United only managing one, to win comfortably.

As First Division Champions, Manchester United were invited to play the F.A.Cup holders in the annual F.A.Charity Shield match and by a strange quirk of fate their opponents were none other than local rivals Manchester City. Played at Maine Road, as Old Trafford was still without floodlights, the 30,495 crowd were rewarded with a somewhat dull match, decided by a solitary Dennis Viollet goal.
It was not, however, completely uneventful. In the 37th minute, United's goalkeeper Ray Wood received an injury and was forced to leave the field. With no substitutes available, Duncan volunteered to squeeze his frame into Wood's jersey and do a stint between the posts.
On the touchline Matt Busby and his backroom staff contemplated what to do, although they would probably have been happy to leave Duncan where he was. However, United's junior goalkeeper, David Gaskell had been seen going into the ground prior to kick off and he was hastily sought out, given a pair of spare boots and sent out onto the Maine Road pitch to face City, relieving Duncan from his custodian duties.
Such was the young stand-ins display, that many thought that Ray Wood had returned to the fray after receiving treatment. As for Duncan, he had added yet another string to his bow and filled yet another position on the football field.

OCTOBER 27TH BLACKPOOL A 2-2

Having lost their unbeaten record the previous Saturday to Everton, United were staring a second consecutive defeat in the face, with Blackpool winning 2-1 with only thirty seconds left to play.
The Seasiders had taken the lead in the 24th minute, somewhat against the run of play, with Durie beating debutant Hawksworth from close in. Taylor put United level and from then on, it was anyones game.

Byrne, who had been in superb form, was caught out of position. Matthews jinked past Duncan and crossed to Mudie who headed home to make it 2-1.

United were now chasing the game and when all looked lost, up popped Tommy Taylor to score an equaliser.

NOVEMBER 3RD WOLVERHAMPTON WANDERERS H 3-0

Back to their winning ways, with an emphatic win over Wolves.

Goals from Whelan and Pegg saw United well in command after only nineteen minutes and the lead should have been increased soon afterwards, but Berry saw his spot kick saved by Finlayson.

Wolves put up a fine defensive display in the second half, but were caught out ten minutes from the end, when Taylor made it 3-0, running on to a long clearance from Wood and outpacing two defenders to score.

NOVEMBER 10TH BOLTON WANDERERS A 0-2

Injuries are part and parcel of the game and despite his ability to look after himself and his strength in the tackle, Duncan was not immune from his share. Following a tussle with Holden on the touchline, he pulled up quickly holding his leg and with assistance from trainer Tom Curry, hobbled off the field.

Following prolonged treatment, he returned to the action, albeit limping badly, and was forced to play wide on the left to prevent much in the way of physical involvement. Pegg moved inside, with Billy Whelan taking Duncan's position in the half back line.

As the game progressed, Duncan moved to centre forward and actually came close to scoring with a header that Hopkinson in the Bolton goal did well to save.

The injury not only curtailed Duncan's involvement, but also upset United's rhythm and towards the end of the first half he was filling the inside forward role.

Following more treatment during the interval, he resumed in his normal left half position and managed to see the game out with the minimum of discomfort.

NOVEMBER 21ST BORUSSIA DORTMUND A 0-0 EUROPEAN CUP 1ST Rnd. 2ND Leg

With a meagre 3-2 advantage, United had to pull out all the stops to remain in the European Cup. In a game played on a frozen pitch, for which the visitors were totally unprepared, having not rubber studs, they withstood considerable pressure to earn a creditable draw which enabled them to progress into the next round.

NOVEMBER 24TH TOTTENHAM HOTSPUR A 2-2

Once again, the name of Duncan Edwards appears in the headlines as he helps a tired looking United side, following their mid-week sojourn to Germany, salvage a point at White Hart Lane. With only a couple of minutes remaining, Duncan, playing at inside left moves wide onto the wing, catching the Tottenham defence flat footed. Receiving the ball from David Pegg, he sets off down the wing and sweeps a fast low cross into the goal mouth, where the oncoming Eddie Colman gratefully accepts the scoring opportunity.

With only minutes remaining the opportunity arose for him to become the match winner, but his tamely hit shot was easily blocked by Ditchburn in the Tottenham goal.

DECEMBER 1ST LUTON TOWN H 3-1

For the second consecutive match, Duncan pulled on the red number ten jersey and straight from the kick off began to cause Luton Town problems. With only four minutes gone, Johnny Berry dribbled through the visiting defence before hitting the ball through the legs of a defender to the feet of Duncan. Without hesitation, even although he was some 25 yards out he sent a searing, left footed shot past Baynham in the Luton goal to give United the lead.

The Luton goalkeeper must have spent a nervous afternoon, as the United inside left fired in shots at every opportunity and at times was extremely lucky not to be beaten. One effort struck the bemused goalkeeper and bounced dangerously around the goalmouth before it was eventually cleared. On a couple of other occasions, he actually wasted good chances by hitting the ball high over the bar.

Duncan's shooting was certainly a major feature of the match against Luton Town, entertaining the crowd and bringing those in the stand to their feet. It didn't, however, please everyone, with one newspaper carrying the headline - "Does England Need Duncan Edwards' Rocket Specials?"

The article that followed, was quite critical of the player and included the following - "Yesterday he seemed to be trying to show the selectors that he's the guy to get goals.

"He turned out at inside left and within four minutes rocketed one into the net. Not only that, he continued firing these rockets throughout the afternoon. "Shoot when you see the whites of their eyes is a good way of going about scoring goals. But not, Duncan, when your colleagues are in a better position."

December 5th saw the Dudley youngster return to familiar territory as an England player, as the World Cup qualifier against Denmark was to be played in the West Midlands, at Wolverhampton Wanderers'

"like some rocket setting off for Mars"...
"almost uprooted the goalpost with a free kick from the edge of the area..."

Molineux ground. There was no special mention in the match programme for the homecoming, but then again, Duncan Edwards needed little in the way of an introduction.

The match itself, was an eventful confrontation and the return to his native surroundings inspired Duncan to one of his best performances in an England jersey, playing at inside left and scoring twice in the 5-2 home victory.

One of the goals was described as being "like some rocket setting off for Mars". Whilst near the end of the match he "almost uprooted the goalpost with a free kick from the edge of the area".

It was not all roses, however, as he gifted Denmark their second goal, allowing them back into the game at 3-2. By the end of the ninety minutes, this slip up was well and truly forgotten, as his overall performance and two goals had erased the memories of the early error.

DECEMBER 8TH ASTON VILLA A 3-1

Duncan returned to his more familiar left half role against Aston Villa, but his couple of games at inside left had prompted much debate as to his actual best position with the letters page of the Manchester Evening News carrying a quite a number of opinions on the subject.

The letter adjudged by the Evening News as being the best on the 'Play Duncan Anywhere' topic was sent in by B.Booth of Eccles and suggested that "Duncan's best position is centre-half and also captain

..."Duncan Edwards is one of the few players who can be utilised in any position without weakening the side"

of the side. He has everything that it takes to follow in the traditions of Stan Cullis and he has it naturally. The physique, speed, ball control, heading ability, fire and dash, adventurous spirit, fearless and above all a natural footballing brain."

B.B. of Salford wrote...."Duncan Edwards is one of the few players who can be utilised in any position without weakening the side."

A.Sanson of Bradford, Manchester 11 said in his letter that "Edwards' combination of physique, stamina. Plus his capacity for playing soccer for the games sake, opens up the possibility that ine day he may have the rare distinction of having a played in every position in the England team. Such is the soccer versatility of Edwards."

G.Eadie of Whitefield wasn't entirely happy about the stopping and changing of positions and wrote - "He is a natural footballer, but that is no justification for playing him in different positions. A versatile player can be moved about so much that he can eventually be moved out of the team.

G.Lock of Chorlton on Medlock summed Duncan up well and suggested like almost all the others that the players best position was left half. He wrote - "Usually big fellows are awkward in controlling the ball. Edwards is the exception. I have seldom seen a player keep up with the play as much as Edwards does. He places the ball accurately and what a shot he has! Play him at left half."

Where he played mattered little to Duncan, as long as he was playing he was happy

DECEMBER 15TH BIRMINGHAM CITY A 1-3

A surprise third defeat of the season.
United never really got out of first gear and struggled to find some co-ordination between defence and attack. Birmingham, on the other hand, made the most of the Champions off day and gave the majority of the 38,600 crowd plenty to shout about.

DECEMBER 26TH CARDIFF CITY H 3-1

A complete reversal of the previous game, with goals from Tyalor, Viollet and Whelan enough to put United back on their winning ways. It was a powerful display in what was surprisingly the highest crowd of the day - 28,607!

DECEMBER 29TH PORTSMOUTH A 3-1

An injury to Tommy Taylor during the Boxing Day fixture against Cardiff City saw United manager Matt Busby surprisingly turn to Duncan in order to fill the vacant number nine shirt, with Wilf McGuinness receiving a rare appearance in the United side as his replacement.
"United banked on 'play anywhere' Duncan Edwards maintaining their Championship drive in his new front role of centre forward" began one of the many reports from the match and as we have been accustomed to over the years, Duncan did not disappoint and thrived in his first League appearance at centre forward.
"Torpedo From Edwards Has Portsmouth All At Sea" proclaimed one of the headlines, but it was not until the second half that he found his goal scoring touch after a handful of missed opportunities in the first forty five minutes.
A desperate challenge had prevented him from opening the scoring early on and in the 11th minute, following a move between Whelan and Viollet, with the latter heading the ball down to the feet of the United makeshift centre forward, the ball was shot hopelessly wide from only eight yards out much to his disgust.
A goal behind at half time, but in a frantic opening to the second half an own goal after only three minutes pulled United back into the game. Five minutes later, they were 2-1 in front, Duncan scoring after fine work from Whelan and Colman. Denis Viollet rounded off a good afternoon's work by scoring the third in the 69th minute.

"Five times this burly youngster, who packs one of the fiercest drives in soccer in his boots, had Portsmouth in dire trouble and because he is Duncan Edwards he was expected to score..."

"Efficiency Edwards" was another of the headlines, with Stan Halsey in his report which followed writing - "Duncan Edwards - left half, inside left and now centre deputising for England colleague Tommy Taylor at centre-forward, yes, Duncan's all right in any position.

"At Portsmouth, he may have lacked Taylor's easy adaptability, especially under the conditions, but a hint of danger lurked behind all he did. Indeed, all the time he was operating, he showed unshakeable confidence. And, it wasn't cockiness."

Other headlines from the newspapers over the following couple of days read "Edwards England's Answer To Charles" and "Edwards Fine Leader" were fitting tributes, but one reporter put things into perspective by writing the following. "The game gave United the opportunity of trying out an experiment everyone wanted to see - the playing of the versatile Duncan Edwards at centre-forward.

"The fact that he easy grace with which the United attack invariably functions was in no way disturbed, and that Edwards scored once and made another goal, made the experiment eminently worthwhile.

"It could quite easily have been sensationally successful if the ball had run just a little more kindly for Edwards in front of goal.

"Five times this burly youngster, who packs one of the fiercest drives in soccer in his boots, had Portsmouth in dire trouble and because he is Duncan Edwards he was expected to score.

"Each time he failed, which doesn't prove anything, except that Edwards is human."

Another reporter commented, that if he were an England selector he would have no hesitation in playing Duncan at centre forward if need be.

JANUARY 1ST CHELSEA H 3-0

As a contest, it was all over four minutes before half time, with United going 3-0 in front.

The second half, surprisingly produced no further goals as United were happy to simply pass the ball around at a leisurely pace, with their minds beginning to focus on their forth coming FA Cup tie.

JANUARY 5TH HARTLEPOOL UNITED A 4-3 FA CUP 3RD RND.

Hartlepool, like Chelsea four days earlier found themselves 3-0 down before they knew what was what, but unlike the London side, the men from the North East were prepared to roll up their sleeves and fight it out with their illustrious visitors.

Two goals, from Whelan and Berry, in the opening eight minutes had put United firmly in the driving seat and a third, from Taylor, in the thirty second minute looked enough to win the game. Hartlepool, however, had other ideas.

Ten minutes before the interval, they had pulled one back and by the sixty fifth minute were, to the delight of their supporters and the dismay of United, on level terms.

Unfortunately, Hartlepool were unable to pull off a major shock no matter how hard they tried and a second goal from Billy Whelan and some desperate defending saw United inch through into the next round.

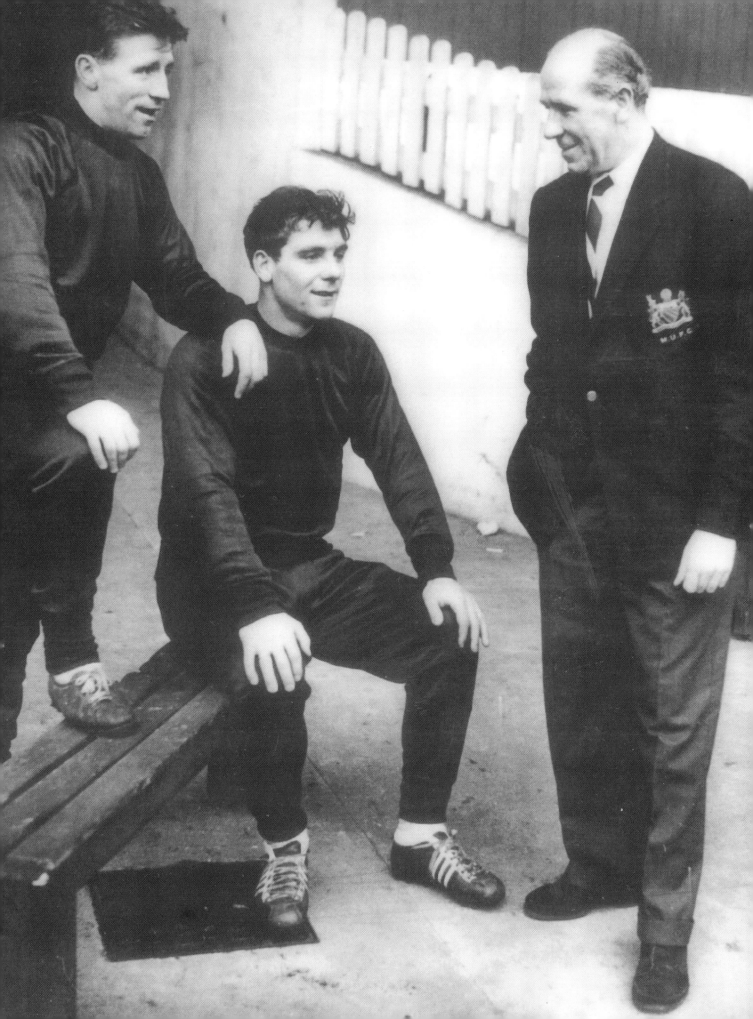

JANUARY 12TH NEWCASTLE UNITED H 6-1

Ideal preparation for the forthcoming trip to Spain came in the 6-1 defeat of Newcastle United. Unlike their North East neighbours Hartlepool, Newcastle were no match for a rampant United side.
United opened the scoring as early as the fifth minute, when Pegg hit the ball home after Duncan's shot had deflected off Whelan and from then on Newcastle were chasing the game.
Further goals from Whelan 2, Viollet 2 and another from Pegg completed the route, with Newcastle grabbing a solitary consolation in the dying minutes.

JANUARY 16TH ATHLETICO BILBAO A 3-5 E. CUP 2ND RND. 1ST LEG

Played in a blizzard, on a sea of mud, United were often outplayed by the tough speedy Spaniards who had a 3-0 half time lead.
Within nine minutes of the re-start, United had pulled two goals back, but soon found themselves again three goals behind when Bilbao went 5-2 in front. A third United goal provided a glimmer of hope for the return leg at Maine Road, but it was going to be a difficult task.

JANUARY 19TH SHEFFIELD WEDNESDAY A 1-2

A surprise defeat at Hillsborough, with perhaps the gruelling trip to Bilbao in mid-week taking more out of the team than they cared to admit.

JANUARY 26TH WREXHAM A 5-0 FA CUP 4TH RND.

Compared to the previous FA Cup tie against Hartlepool, there was never any doubt regarding the out come of this fourth round tie in North Wales.

"He was a magnificent exhibition of hard constructive play"

Goals from Whelan 2, Taylor2 and a Roger Byrne penalty settled the tie, with Duncan as always in the heart of the action. "The strong man in Manchester United's half back line" wrote one of the many reporters covering the match. "He was a magnificent exhibition of hard constructive play."

FEBRUARY 2ND MANCHESTER CITY A 4-2

The games were now coming thick and fast. League, FA Cup, European Cup and of course Army representative games all featuring on Duncan's fixture list. But for sheer excitement and a hard fought ninety minutes few could compare with a 'derby' match against neighbours Manchester City.

The Maine Road fixture flew from end to end and there was little to judge between the two sides. With the game delicately poised at 3-2 in United's favour and only ten minutes left to play, David Pegg found Duncan with a throw in, just inside the City penalty area. His shot, not one of his more powerful efforts, spun past goalkeeper Bert Trautmann and into the net. 4-2 to United. The points were now safe.

FEBRUARY 6TH ATHLETICO BILBAO H 3-0 E. CUP 2ND RND. 2ND LEG

With so much to do in order to claw their way back into the game, it was not surprising that United began more than a little nervously. The crowd too began to feel the strain as the first half neared a goal less end.

From his position on the touch line, Matt Busby sent instructions to Duncan to move further forward and help his attack. No sooner had they been received, than Duncan proceeded up-field like a runaway tank and succeeded in getting a shot in on goal which the Bilbao 'keeper could only block with his foot. A lurking Dennis Viollet scored with the rebound. Three minutes before the interval, United were back in the game, the deadlock was broken.

As the second half progressed, United saw two goals disallowed for offside, before Taylor scored the equaliser. It was all to play for now. The crowd, however, were kept on tender hooks until five minutes from time when Johnny Berry concluded one of United's best ever performances by scoring a third goal, ensuring their passage into the next round.

FEBRUARY 9TH ARSENAL H 6-2

Another three points in the quest for a second consecutive League Championship, with Arsenal failing to offer much in the way of resistance, as United maintained their position at the top of the table with 44 points from 28 games. Four points in front of Tottenham Hotspur.

Still not noted for his goal scoring ability, Duncan for the first time in his career, found the back of the net in consecutive League fixtures, scoring United's third of the afternoon.

Whelan, wide on the left, squared the ball inside to the United left half. Moving forward, he brushed aside a couple of Arsenal challenges before putting everything behind a shot from eight yards out which flew into the net.

Near the end, he almost added another, but this time, Kelsey in the Arsenal goal was equal to it and turned the ball round the post for a corner.

Despite an important FA Cup 5th round tie looming on the horizon, Duncan was back at his Army barracks, fit and therefore available for selection for an Army Cup semi-final.

As the match progressed, the England internationalist's team were obviously not enjoying the best of afternoon's as they trailed 4-2. Mid-way through the second half and no breakthrough looking likely, Duncan asked for permission to move from left half to inside left. This was granted and the outcome of the cup-tie suddenly changed.

In a matter of fourteen and a half minutes, he had scored five goals and earned his team a place in the Final.

FEBRUARY 16TH EVERTON H 1-0 FA CUP 5TH RND.

The Goodison Park side were proving stern opposition for United, with the opening forty-five minutes failing to produce any goals. The opinion around Old Trafford during the interval was that the second period was likely to turn out the same way as both teams were giving very little away.

..."the big left half was a one man power house for United and his golden goal capped four previous worthy scoring efforts"

As the second half progressed, Duncan was the driving force behind United's search for the illusive goal and it came as no surprise when he eventually made the breakthrough in the 67th minute.

Berry, not for the first time, was the provider wide on the right and his cross field ball found Whelan in a promising position. The Irishman's shot, however, was crowded out. The ball then ran loose to the feet of Duncan Edwards, on the edge of the area, who quickly brought it under control before hitting a right footed shot just inside the Everton post for what turned out to be the only goal of the game.

Frank Smith, in the News Of The World, wrote - "It was fitting that Duncan Edwards should score the match winner, for the big left half was a one man power house for United and his golden goal capped four previous worthy scoring efforts."

FEBRUARY 23RD BLACKPOOL H 0-2

A disappointing afternoon all round, with the Seasiders inflicting United's first home defeat since October 20th when Everton won 5-2 and only their third since March 1955, ironically also against Everton.

It was reported that Duncan "played like two men", but he could do little to prevent the visitors taking both points. He came close to scoring near the end, when along with Pegg, tried to force the ball over the line after hitting the post, but the referee turned down his appeals for a goal.

MARCH 2ND BOURNEMOUTH A 2-1 FA CUP 6TH RND.

An injury to Tommy Taylor, once again saw Matt Busby turn to Duncan in his hour of need and select him at centre forward for a difficult cup-tie on the south coast at Bournemouth. The move, however,

"No one had greater drive than Duncan Edwards"

was to be short lived, as an injury to Mark Jones after only ten minutes forced the makeshift centre forward into becoming the stand in centre half.

Shortly after moving into the defensive position he was almost caught out, as he hesitated on the ball, when he had all the time in the world to clear. Bedford, the Bournemouth centre forward saw his chance, nipped in and took the ball of his foot and sent a shot from all of twenty yards crashing against the bar much to the relief of a red faced Duncan Edwards.

Bournemouth continued to make life difficult for United and in the end, the First division side were grateful to Johnny Berry for his two goals, which them a place in the semi-final for the first time since 1949.

According to the bookmakers, United were now at 5 to 1 to win the League Championship, FA Cup and the European Cup. A difficult task, but one that was certainly not beyond them and more than one eager supporter gladly accepted the odds as a fair bet.

The fixture against Everton at Goodison Park on March 6th found Duncan, along with Bill Foulkes, Eddie Colman and Bobby Charlton all missing, as they had been selected to play for the Army against the RAF, in a crunch match at that level the previous evening. Thankfully their omission from the United side did not prove costly, as their stand ins coped favourably and helped United to another two vital points with a 2-1 win.

MARCH 9TH ASTON VILLA H 1-1

Returned to the United line up as centre forward, surprisingly taking over from Colin Webster who had scored both United goals in the 2-1 victory over Everton three days previously.

Having started the game leading the line, he was largely employed in a wandering role, which did little to help United's overall performance in a rather disappointing 1-1 draw.

Duncan did find the net in the 65th minute, but saw his effort disallowed for offside.

MARCH 16TH WOLVERHAMPTON WANDERERS A 1-1

Back to left half for the trip to his home territory, which saw his schoolboy friend Gordon Clayton make his League debut.

Not surprisingly, Duncan played more of a defensive role, helping his friend through a difficult fixture. He cleared one goal bound shot off the line and did well to protect his goalkeeper.

MARCH 23RD BIRMINGHAM CITY A 2-0 FA CUP SEMI FINAL

With a place in the FA Cup Final at stake, Birmingham City found Duncan and his team mates in typical dominating form, with United taking a 2-0 first half lead with goals from Berry and Charlton.
"No one had greater drive than Duncan Edwards" reported one of the newspapers, as the United left half did the work of two men. One minute he was clearing his lines, the next he was setting up an attack. His defensive qualities were certainly appreciated on one occasion when he prevented a certain goal, kicking clear, after Ray Wood dropped the ball following a corner kick.
Despite some pressure from the Midlands side, whom United had not beaten this season, the two first half goals were enough to see them through to the Wembley Final.

MARCH 25TH BOLTON WANDERERS H 0-2

It was back to centre forward for Duncan for the visit of Bolton Wanderers to Old Trafford for what was the first fixture played under floodlights at the ground.
In his report for the Guardian, Don Davies, 'An Old International' wrote, "Edwards was labouring heavily at centre forward, though staining to pull his weight like a willing dray horse. It cannot be said that he was receiving too much support from the others." He was later to add, "Hopkinson in the Wanderers' goal saved brilliantly from Berry and Edwards. One shot in particular from Edwards spurted upwards from the goalkeeper's foot almost to the height of the illumination towers."
United were two down after 49 minutes and with only a quarter of an hour to play, Duncan was moved back to centre half, with Jackie Blanchflower taking up the right wing position in a re-shuffled forward line, but to no avail.

MARCH 30TH LEEDS UNITED A 2-1

Another two hard earned points in the quest for the illusive treble and it wasn't until three minutes from the end that the points were secured in controversial fashion.
Berry, who had already given United a 34th minute lead, swung a corner into the Leeds goalmouth where the ball was apparently handled by Duncan prior to Whelan having a shot at goal. The Leeds goalkeeper failed to hold the ball and a grateful Bobby Charlton accepted the scoring opportunity without a second thought.

Saturday April 6th saw Duncan make a pre-Cup Final appearance at Wembley as a member of the England team to face old rivals Scotland.

To the delight of the many Scottish supporters sprinkled around the packed Stadium the visitors took the lead after only sixty seconds through Ring. England, although shaken by the early goal, quickly fought back, and it was Duncan who came closest to an equaliser. Following a foul on Finney by Docherty, his Preston team mate, some five or six yards outside the penalty area, he could only stand a watch as his free kick flashed past the join of the post and crossbar.

Scotland almost went 2-0 in front, when England goalkeeper Hodgkinson misjudged a free kick from Ring, but was grateful to find Duncan positioned on the goal line and able to clear.

England eventually equalised through Derek Kevan and the match took on an extra edge, with tackles having an added bite as players put more determination into their play. Ducan found himself a target for a series of boo's from the Scottish support following a rather heavy tackle on Fernie. He did little to endear himself further to the tartan clad followers with seven minutes to go.

Killing the slight bounce of the ball some twenty-five yards out, he hit the piece of leather from something of an angle towards the Scottish goal where Younger had absolutely no chance in saving the shot due to its exceptional speed. The match was won, with Duncan both the hero and villain of the afternoon.

APRIL 11TH REAL MADRID A 1-3 E. CUP SEMI FINAL 1ST LEG

United's European Cup hopes suffered a severe blow at the hands of the Spanish maestro's, who had the likes of Di Stefano, Mateos, Rial and Kopa in their side, all highly experienced players. The

..."a superb all round display"...

..."Salute Duncan Edwards who, if he made no impact in attack, performed noble deeds of daring in defence"

performance of the referee did not help United much, with many decisions going against them, but Duncan perhaps hit the nail on the head with his after match statement - "We simply did not get going until Real Madrid went 2-0 in front and by then it was a little too late."

Although certainly disappointed with the overall team performance, Duncan could feel happy about his own during a testing ninety minutes. "Like a tank at left half" said one report, while another contained "a superb all round display". Henry Rose, in the Daily Express wrote - "Salute Duncan Edwards who, if he made no impact in attack, performed noble deeds of daring in defence."

He was, however, spoken to by the referee early in the game for a rather robust challenge and if he could not understand what the Dutch referee was saying, he certainly had no difficulty in picking up his gestures.

United certainly had it all to do in the second leg at Old Trafford.

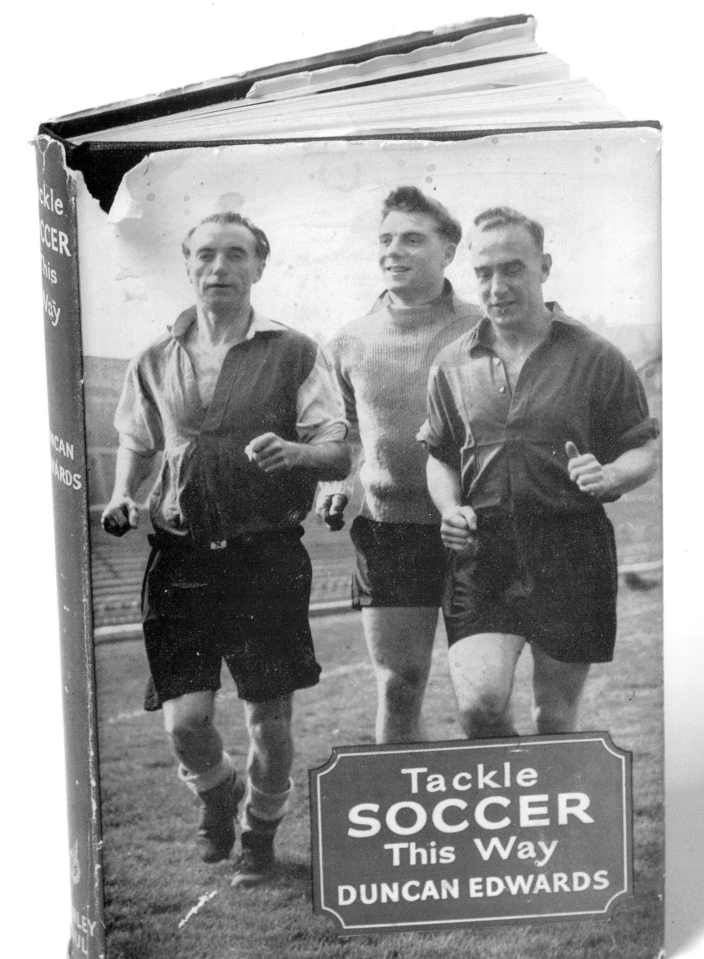

Tackle
SOCCER
This Way
DUNCAN EDWARDS

APRIL 13TH LUTON TOWN A 2-0

The final few hurdles in the Championship race were in sight and the awkward away trip to Luton and subsequent fixtures would all be treated like Cup Final's until the title was secured.

Despite some brave defending by the home side, Duncan finally managed to prize it open, setting up the opening goal for Tommy Taylor in the 52nd minute. A second goal, by the same player, twenty-five minutes later killed the game and Luton's hopes of an equaliser.

With only three minutes remaining, Duncan almost added a third, with a repeat of his match winning effort against Scotland the previous Saturday. Having been awarded a free-kick just outside the Luton penalty area, Duncan smashed a mighty left foot drive against the post, which was almost snapped in two by the ferocity of the shot.

This victory kept United firmly in top position with 55 points from 37 games. Preston were second, four points behind, with Blackpool a further two behind in third.

APRIL 19TH BURNLEY A 3-1

Burnley's first home defeat for a year came courteously of a Billy Whelan hat trick, with Duncan keeping a close watch over danger man Jimmy McIlroy.

The home side had a chance to equalise with the score at 2-1, but missed a penalty. The overall result, however, was never in any real doubt.

APRIL 20TH SUNDERLAND H 4-0

With three games still to play, United were crowned First Division Champions for the second consecutive season. An early goal, in the sixth minute, from Billy Whelan set United on their way and a second from the same player in the 76th minute left the outcome of the match, and the title, in any doubt.

Four minutes later, Duncan added a third, collecting the ball some thirty yards out and hitting it high into the Sunderland net with a real blockbuster of a shot. Taylor added a fourth, one minute from time.

APRIL 25TH REAL MADRID H 2-2 E.CUP SEMI FINAL 2ND LEG

United fought to reverse the balance of the tie as they had done against Madrid's Spanish rivals Athletico Bilbao. The game, however, turned into a rather untidy affair, with Duncan and his captain, Roger Byrne, incited into actions that they would want to forget.

As the game and the hopes of a place in the Final slowly slipped away from United, Duncan lost his cool and in one incident, attempted to drag the injured Manuel Torres off the pitch so that the game could be re-started.

Madrid, as in the first leg, took a 2-0 lead before United could really get going and their second half revival was once again too little too late.

MAY 4TH ASTON VILLA A 1-2 FA CUP FINAL.

There was to be no League and FA Cup double for United as an injury to goalkeeper Ray Wood, following a collision with Villa's McParland, forced a complete re-shuffle with Jackie Blanchflower taking over in goal (and performing heroically), Duncan moving to centre half and a dazed Ray Wood wandering helplessly on the wing. This certainly reduced United's attacking options with Duncan having remain more or less constantly in defence.

McParland was involved in more controversy following Villa's second goal in the 72nd minute, five minutes after giving his side the lead. Clearly in an off side position when Myerscough's shot hit the United crossbar with Blanchflower beaten, he collected the rebound and fired home.

With six minutes remaining, a corner, United's 10th in the second half, taken by Duncan was headed home by Taylor and despite an instant re-shuffle with Wood returning to his familiar goalkeeping position, United just could not force the sought for equaliser. The chance of the League and Cup double had gone.

..."He tackled strongly and fairly, broke up repeated Villa attacks..."

In his report for the Daily Express, Henry Rose wrote- "Duncan Edwards was not the giant he was when pressed to play at centre half at Bournemouth in the FA Cup.

"He tackled strongly and fairly, broke up repeated Villa attacks, but did not make the impact on the game I thought he would in United's heartbreaking uphill struggle."

Obviously disappointed, Duncan commented after the match that "I felt very tired midway through the second half. It had thrown a big responsibility on our ten man team. Villa's two quick goals shook us and even after Tommy Taylor scored, I still felt we might get the equaliser.

Despite a gruelling domestic season, Duncan could not yet put away his boots and enjoy a leisurely couple of months with his girl friend Molly Leach, as he still had five fixtures to fulfil at International level. Three were with the full international side, World Cup ties against the Republic of Ireland twice and Denmark, due to be played in a eleven day period, with under 23 outings against Rumania and Czechoslovakia.

The first in the trio of World Cup fixtures, on May 8th against the Republic of Ireland at Wembley, attracted only around 52,000 spectators, who saw England outclass the visitors 5-1.

The match was over by half time, with England 3-1 in front and as the fixture was played out at something of a practise match pace Duncan enjoyed a somewhat leisurely afternoon compared to recent fixtures.

Seven days later in Copenhagen, England followed up their 5-2 victory at Wolverhampton against the Danes with a 4-1 win. The home side surprisingly scored first and it was not until the final twenty minutes that Duncan and his team mates gained the upper hand.

There was a four day break before the visit to Dalymount Park and the return against the Irish and in front of a packed stadium, the Republic side put up a much more spirited display than they had done at Wembley. Duncan had his hands full, being up against his United team mate Billy Whelan and in the tightly fought contest the honours were shared in a 1-1 draw.

Following the World Cup tie in Dublin, Duncan was off on his travels once again, catching a flight to Bucharest to join up with his under 23 team mates for the remaining two games of a three game mini-tour.

During the flight to the Rumanian capital, Duncan became slightly nervous and worried as he looked out the small window beside him. Flying almost alongside, and in his eyes a bit too close for comfort, was a MIG fighter plane. The plane was possibly on some routine training mission, but for lance-corporal Edwards, who remember was not the best of traveller's, it was not what you would expect to see when thousands of feet above the ground looking out across the sky.

Upon landing at Bucharest airport and reaching the team hotel, he bumped into Daily Express correspondent Bob Pennington, who, during their conversation asked about the journey out. The still nervous Duncan related his experience regarding the fighter plane to the newspaper man, who was obviously more than interested in the story. His plans for an excellent exclusive were, however, quickly thwarted, as Duncan swore Pennington to secrecy and managed to persuade him not to print the story in case there were any serious repercussions, causing problems with the tour.

The incident was soon put to the back of Duncan's mind as he got down to the business in hand.

In Bucharest, he set up the only goal of the game for Johnny Haynes, whilst in the second fixture against Czechoslovakia in Bratislava, he scored both England goals in a 2-0 victory.

The journey home was obviously quite tense, with occasional glances out over the skyline, but there was no repeat sightings and the matter was soon forgotten as Duncan went off to enjoy a delayed close season break.

CHAPTER SEVEN
IT ALL ENDED IN TEARS

On June 6th, at 2pm, 23145376 Lance Corporal Edwards was officially demobilised from the army, although his name would still appear on the list of reserves, should an emergency ever materialise.

Even although Duncan was one of the 'big name' player's in the game at that particular time, the event was rather surprisingly covered in the national press, with the 'Daily Express' carrying a special 'Photo News' feature, under the heading - 'A Soldier End's Double Life. From Now On It's Soccer.'

The article, which was accompanied by a selection of photographs, said : "..at 2 o'clock yesterday, he stopped being a 9/- (45p) a day "Lance Jack" and became once again the full time soccer star said to be worth £50,000 in the European Common Market - Soccer Branch."

Upon finishing his stint in the army, Duncan commented that he was naturally glad that his national service was over, but that he had been treated marvellously and had no complaints.

One point worth noting regarding Duncan's national service is the fact that during his two year stint in the army, he played over 180 matches. And today's top players think they have it hard!

AUGUST 24TH LEICESTER CITY A 3-0

An excellent start to the season and the retention of the First Division title, with Billy Whelan scoring a hat trick.

"The accuracy with which Duncan Edwards sprayed his passes, both long and short was almost uncanny"

In defence, Duncan was supreme, continuing where he had left off in the pre-season friendlies in Germany, where the German public appreciated his dynamic performances. He robbed Leicester City of countless of scoring opportunities with important tackles and was also widely praised for his first class distribution, with one reporter writing "The accuracy with which Duncan Edwards sprayed his passes, both long and short was almost uncanny".

AUGUST 28TH EVERTON H 3-0

Goals from Tommy Taylor, Dennis Viollet and an Everton own goal maintained United's 100% record in a match that saw the opposition cause few problems.

AUGUST 31ST MANCHESTER CITY H 4-1

"Duncan Edwards Hits Home a 25 yard Special"

"Duncan Edwards Hits Home a 25 yard Special" proclaimed the headlines in the Manchester Evening Chronicle. Alf Clarke, in his report underneath wrote of United's first goal : "Racing through, Duncan Edwards took a pass from Billy Whelan and from 25 yards drove the ball just inside the post past Trautmann in the City goal."

Having sprang City's attempted offside trap for the opening goal, he continued to be a thorn in their side for the rest of the afternoon and was a tower of strength in both defence and attack. He was booed by the City supporters in the crowd for a foul on Barlow but it was to little effect. Later in the game took over from Jackie Blanchflower in the heart of the United defence when the Irishman got injured and did his usual reliable stand in job.

SEPTEMBER 4TH EVERTON A 3-3

It looked as if it was going to be a repeat of the match at Old Trafford seven days previously, with United 2-0 in front at half time. However, an injury to Jackie Blanchflower upset the rhythm and Everton fought back to earn a draw.

SEPTEMBER 7TH LEEDS UNITED H 5-0

Back to the winning ways, with a five goal romp against the Yorkshire side. Berry 2, Taylor 2 and Viollet the scorers, making it 18 goals for and only four against after only five games of the new season.

SEPTEMBER 9TH BLACKPOOL A 4-1

United continued their superb start to the season turning in a devastating display at Bloomfield Road, with Duncan once again taking up more ink from the reporters pens than the rest of his team mates put together.

Archie Ledbrooke was to write - "Duncan Edwards at his majestic best and therefore nearly the best player in the world. One minute he was clearing off his own goal line, the next he was running through half the Blackpool side in a solo dash that owed as much to artistry as it did to shear strength."

Ledbrooke's fellow reporter Terence Elliott wrote - "Before the thunder and roll of the Champions fanfare had died, Whelan back heels the ball to Edwards, for the young giant to hammer a drive that almost breaks an upright in two."

SEPTEMBER 14TH BOLTON WANDERERS A 0-4

A real local 'derby' with neither side giving a quarter and Duncan well in the thick of things. On the half-hour his will to win was more than apparent, when he left his second cousin, Bolton's Dennis Stevens, limping on the wing following one particularly hard challenge.

The Bolton player tried to hit a pass to team-mate Birch, as Duncan moved in to block the ball and in the inevitable collision, Stevens was left writhing in agony on the touchline and had to be carried off on a stretcher.

He returned after treatment, but had a noticeable limp, but this did not make him immune from further involvement. Shortly afterwards, he again came face to face with Duncan and once again came off the worst, another crunching tackle leaving him prostrate on the ground. Upon his recovery, the two players were seen to exchange some not too friendly words. Stevens's team mate Ball also came off worse in a tackle with United's man mountain and spent some time in obvious agony.

SEPTEMBER 18TH BLACKPOOL H 1-2

Revenge they say is sweet, so Blackpool must have enjoyed their 2-1 win against United at Old Trafford following their 4-1 home defeat nine days previously.

United's solitary effort came from Duncan, who had numerous shots on target before he eventually found the back of the net.

..."Duncan Edwards at last got one through...
..."it tested the net as no inspecting referee could"

Duncan's shooting had caused numerous goalkeepers nightmares and his latest goal, despite not being a match winning effort was described as follows, "As he was determined to do, Duncan Edwards at last got one through in the 87th minute, one that even the agile, experienced George Farm could scarcely have seen, near though it went to him, before it tested the net as no inspecting referee could."

SEPTEMBER 21ST ARSENAL H 4-2

An interesting fixture tactic wise, with Duncan playing a double centre half role alongside Jackie Blanchflower in an effort to control Arsenal's twin threat of David Herd and Vic Groves.

The ploy certainly paid off, with United running out clear winners, thanks to goals from Taylor, Pegg and a Whelan double.

SEPTEMBER 25TH SHAMROCK ROVERS A 6-0 EUROPEAN CUP RND

United had a let off in the opening minute when the home side almost scored, but after that it was one way traffic as United set out to make amends for the disappointment of losing out to Real Madrid in last seasons competition.

SEPTEMBER 28TH WOLVERHAMPTON WANDERERS A 1-3

A third defeat in four games brought some criticism of Busby's team selection, which saw Wilf McGuinness fill the unfamiliar left back slot. As the youngster was having a clearly uncomfortable afternoon, the question was asked to why Duncan had not been pushed back, with McGuinness filling a more familiar half back role?

The second leg of the European Cup tie against Shamrock Rovers and the league fixture, also at Old Trafford, against Aston Villa three days later were both missed by Duncan due to a bout of flu. Both games were fortunately won in his absence. The European tie 3-2 and the League fixture 4-1, with Wilf McGuinness the replacement on both occasions.

OCTOBER 12TH NOTTINGHAM FOREST A 2-1

The members of the nations press must have enjoyed reporting on United games, which allowed them to scour their dictionary's in search of adjectives to describe Duncan and his displays. The latest collection came following the victory at Forest's City Ground, when the following was penned - "It was only 22 carat display's from Ray Wood, Roger Byrne and that chasing, crunching, man mountain Duncan Edwards that stopped Billy Walker's boy's from collecting the points."

..."that hunk of excellence Duncan Edwards, the most effective one-man performer in British football."

Desmond Hackett in the Daily Express wrote - "Forest's swift well drilled forward routine demanded only the best from goalkeeper and that hunk of excellence Duncan Edwards, the most effective one-man performer in British football".
"Both Forest and United were brilliant", wrote another scribe of the time, "with Manchester having the extra edge which brought victory. That extra edge was the tremendous performance of Duncan Edwards, the young giant at left half. He kept popping up like a hero of a film serial to save his side from disaster".
In the Times, their man at the match wrote - "Yet one man stood out above all others. He was Duncan Edwards, now more than usual guarding the backward areas around Blanchflower. His was a massive performance."

No sooner had he got back into the United side following his two match enforced absence, than he was missing again. This time, however, it was because of England duty and an international against Wales at Cardiff.

Manager of the Welsh side of that time was of course Jimmy Murphy. In his book 'Matt, United and Me', published by Souvenir Press in 1968, Jimmy recalled this particular match in a chapter all about Duncan. He wrote: "I had gone through our tactics to play England. I dealt with all aspects, until Reg Davies, the very talented Newcastle United and Welsh inside forward, who was a very good player for one so small and frail, piped up: "You have mentioned everyone Jimmy, but what about Duncan Edwards?" "Just keep out of his way son", I said, "I don't want you to get hurt."

"Edwards nonchalantly picked off Davis and all others as if they were flies. And he did it all almost at walking pace."

Neither Davies or any of his team mates caused England any problems that afternoon and as the minutes ticked away with England leading 4-0, Duncan, whilst preparing to take a throw in quipped to Murphy, sitting along the touchline on the Welsh bench, "Are there no early trains back to Manchester Jimmy, as you are certainly wasting your time here."

"I'll see you later and tell you where you are going wrong", came the reply from the Welshman.

"A young oak" wrote the Times correspondent, who continued, "Edwards nonchalantly picked off Davis and all others as if they were flies. And he did it all almost at walking pace."

The Manchester United side of this time were a close knit group of individuals, who were fond of each others company. Roger Byrne was perhaps the exception to the rule, not for any reason other than the fact that he was studying physiotherapy. He was of course also married, whilst the others were single and slightly younger.

After training, the likes of Duncan, Eddie Colman, David Pegg , Wilf McGuinness and Bobby Charlton would pass the time by listening to the latest records at each others homes or digs, whilst a Saturday night would find them out on the town, either with their girlfriends or in a group together enjoying the Manchester and Salford night spots, with admission to most venues free to the familiar faces.

In those distant days, you trained and played football and that was it. There was little in the way of outside demands on the players like there is for the professionals of today. Few had any interests away from the game.

Some of the more seasoned players opened shops, hoping that their name alone would attract custom. Others were considered to have a name, which would attract readership to particular newspapers if they put their names to a "ghost written" column.

Duncan certainly had a marketable name and it was not surprising that attempts were made at exploiting it in a minor way.

The Manchester Evening Chronicle approached him regarding a weekly column in their 'Saturday Pink' edition, which he accepted, with his thoughts on all football matters eagerly digested by the readers. Advertising was another area where the name of Duncan Edwards was soon to be found, with his photograph appearing on an advert for 'Dextrosol' glucose tablets.

Alongside his photograph was written, "Manchester United's great discovery and, at 18, the youngest player for fifty years to win a full cap for England says - "Playing in top gear until the final whistle can really take it out of you. That's why I find 'Dextrosol' glucose tablets so handy. They're a natural source of energy you can rely on anytime, anywhere."

Anyone who had seen Duncan play knew only too well that he did not need 'Dextrosol' to see him through a game and whether or not he did enjoy the odd tablet or two before a match or at half time was anybody's guess. There is little doubt, however, that 'Dextrosol' would have enjoyed an upsurge in sales due to Duncan's involvement.

His column in the Manchester Evening Chronicle rarely raised much in the way of debate, but in the issue of October 5th, the content did raise a few eyebrows and became a topic of much conversation in the pubs around Manchester that particular Saturday night.

"Italian's Haven't Made Me An Offer."

"Italian's Haven't Made Me An Offer" screamed the headlines and the sentences which followed were eagerly read by all.

"In common with Tommy Taylor and most of the other star footballers in this country, my name has been linked with Italian football. Right now I should like to say that there has been no official approach to me, and, if there were, I should refer it immediately to United manager Matt Busby. I would regard such a situation as club business, and, after they had made up their minds, I might be in a position to consider it." There was, however, little danger of United allowing Duncan, or any of their players for that matter, leave the club.

As something of celebrities, there were occasions when the United player's were asked to present prizes at local functions, and of course, were always happy to oblige. A local Boy's Club asked if Duncan could present the trophies following a five-a-side tournament and he declared that he was only to happy to do so. However, he was later to discover that five of his junior United colleagues were actually playing in the competition and he was quickly into Matt Busby's office to ask if there was any possibility that he could play ? "I am only 21" came his reasoning. Needless to say that his request was denied. Imagine, the most talked about player in the country playing in a Boy's Club five-a-side competition!

OCTOBER 26TH WEST BROMWICH ALBION A 3-4

A defensive mix up between Duncan and Goodwin gave Robson Albion's equaliser to make the score 2-2. An enthralling match, serving up 90 minutes of first class entertainment for the 52,160 crowd. United opened the scoring through Tommy Taylor, but the home side soon equalised through Bobby Robson. Taylor once again put United in front, only for a mix up between Duncan and Goodwin to present

Robson with a second equaliser. Kevin then proceeded to give Albion the lead just before half time. Seventeen minutes after the interval it was 4-2 to the home side, Allen the scorer on this occasion. United, however, never gave up trying and pulled it back to 4-3 in the 76th minute through Whelan, but it was not enough, as the home side held on to the end.

NOVEMBER 2ND BURNLEY H 1-0

Following an indifferent performance against West Bromwich Albion, Duncan was back to his best against Burnley, with a headline proclaiming - "Burnley Blasted By Edwards".

"United beat Burnley because of Edwards..." ..."He spoon fed his colleagues and inspired them."

"United beat Burnley because of Duncan Edwards" the corresponding report began. "He reached peak form and was the complete footballer - the pillar which held up United - well worth £60,000, whether Italian lira or pounds sterling. Powerful in defence with his amazing facility of turning defence into attack. He spoon fed his colleagues and inspired them."

He also made the United goal for Tommy Taylor, with a fine interchanged of passes, before heading the ball into the path of the United centre forward who scored with a right footed shot.

But it was in the final thrusts that Duncan set a brilliant example. Every time he got the ball and ploughed through with it, the crowd roared with excitement. Three times he was foiled by shell shocked Burnley defenders who went into the path of his powerful shots.

On one other occasion, he raced through, beating two or three Burnley defenders in the process, before hitting a terrific shot. The ball struck a defender, bounced upwards, beating the Burnley goalkeeper, struck the bar and then went behind for a corner.

On November 6th, Duncan was in the England side to face Northern Ireland at Wembley, where a superb goalkeeping display by Harry Gregg, then of Doncaster Rovers but soon to become a team mate of Duncan's at Old Trafford, saw Northern Ireland earn a superb victory.

The Irish took the lead through a McIlroy penalty after half an hour, but shortly after the interval A'Court equalised. Twenty minutes later, however, Ireland were 3-1 in front due to poor play by the England defence.

Gregg performed heroics as England attempted to get back into the game, but with only ten minutes to play he could do little to prevent Duncan pulling the game back to 3-2 following a fine pass from Douglas. There were no further goals, as the Irish defence held firm for the remainder of the game.

SOCCER EXPERTS SAY—

extra energy makes the difference!

DUNCAN EDWARDS

Manchester United's great discovery and, at 18, the youngest player for fifty years to win a full cap for England, says:

"Playing in top gear until the final whistle can really take it out of you. That's why I find 'Dextrosol' Glucose Tablets so handy. They're a natural source of energy you can rely on, anytime, anywhere."

Dextrosol
gives extra energy

To produce energy, your body burns fuel. A doctor will tell you that glucose is the fuel manufactured by your body from the food you eat. 'Dextrosol' is pure glucose: the quick, *natural* source of energy. 'Dextrosol' requires no digestion but passes straight into your bloodstream, carrying energy at once to muscles, nerves and brain.

To build up energy for that extra effort, to replace energy after exertion, eat delicious 'Dextrosol' Glucose Tablets. The handy packets slip easily into your pocket. 'Dextrosol' is the natural way of renewing energy—it can do you nothing but good, and there's no limit to the amount you can eat.

For extra energy—whenever you need it!

Look for the handy red and green packets, 11½d. and 6d. Buy a packet today— 'Dextrosol' Glucose Tablets are now available at chemists and grocers everywhere!

DEXTROSOL
glucose tablets
FOR EXTRA ENERGY

DEXTROSOL glucose tablets
BRAND

NOVEMBER 9TH PRESTON NORTH END A 1-1

The visit to Preston's Deepdale ground, did not produce the best of starts, with Duncan giving away a penalty kick in the second minute. He was judged by the referee to have handled a centre from Mayers, but protested is innocence profoundly. Justice was done, however, when Wood not only blocked Finney's spot kick, but also the resulting rebound from Mayers.

The home side did eventually take the lead and indeed looked capable of obtaining both points. Duncan thought that he had scored the equaliser, in the 78th minute. He gained possession when the ball was lobbed through and ran forward before beating Else in the Preston goal with a low shot. The referee was immediately surrounded by protesting North End players and after a brief consultation with his linesman, disallowed the goal for offside.

Whelan eventually did snatch an equaliser for United, with the game looking lost.

NOVEMBER 16TH SHEFFIELD WEDNESDAY H 2-1

Two Colin Webster goals were enough to over come Sheffield Wednesday in a closely fought match in front of almost 41,000 at Old Trafford.

NOVEMBER 20TH DUKLA PRAGUE H 3-0 E.CUP 1ST RND. 1ST LEG

"For United, the real hero was once again Duncan Edwards"...
..."From the first minute to the last, he was wonderful"...

"For United, the real hero was once again Duncan Edwards", wrote the Times reporter at the match. "From the first minute to the last, he was wonderful. There was no other word for him. He was an express train in full cry, always under control, always influencing affairs, always a danger whenever in possession.

"It was a snorting shot of his from some 25 yards out that brought the Czechoslovakian goalkeeper full length to a great save that probably gave United the first signal to go about their duty."

Following missed penalty kicks by both Roger Byrne and Johnny Berry, in was announced that any further spot kicks awarded to United would be taken by Duncan. Apparently in preparation for such an event, he had been eagerly practising his penalty kicks and reportedly had shown little inclination to place the ball, instead preferring to blast it with as much effort as possible, giving the goalkeeper as little chance as possible of stopping the shot.

NOVEMBER 23RD NEWCASTLE UNITED A 2-1

A rather sluggish game, which saw Newcastle United leading 1-0 at the interval. Manager Matt Busby then decided to switch Duncan and inside right Billy Whelan in the hope that the latter's strength would be able force something out of the game.

Slowly, United began to dominate play, with Duncan at the forefront of everything. The breakthrough eventually came, with five minutes to go, when Tommy Taylor opened the Newcastle defence with a fine through pass from the edge of the area. Duncan gathered the ball in his stride and rounded the advancing Simpson, before firing the ball home.

Play flowed from end to end as both sides went for what could turn out to be the winning goal and as it began to look as though a draw was going to be the final result, Tommy Taylor scored with only two minutes remaining.

Following the surprise defeat against Northern Ireland, England got back to their winning ways with a 4-0 victory over France. Goals came from debutant Bobby Robson and United's Tommy Taylor, scoring two apiece, with the England defence having a commanding match.

NOVEMBER 30TH TOTTENHAM HOTSPUR H 3-4

In the first skirmish, Duncan received a kick on the leg and for some time afterwards was seen to be limping.

Tottenham were by far the better team, with the United forward line showing little productivity, due to the visitors good defensive work, especially in their ploy to keep Duncan outwith possible shooting range.

As the minutes ticked away, he did manage a couple of shots as the Tottenham defence relaxed a little with the points secure. His attempts, however, caused little concern, with one from quite far out almost hitting the floodlight pylon.

DECEMBER 4TH DUKLA PRAGUE A 0-1 E.CUP 1ST RND. 2ND LEG

A poor team performance, gave Dukla some hope of salvaging something from the tie, but they could only muster a solitary goal and United hang on to go through to the next round on a 3-1 aggregate win. A collision of heads with a Dukla forward seemed to affect his overall game.

DECEMBER 7TH BIRMINGHAM CITY A 3-3

No Czechoslovakian hangover, as United shared six goals in an end to end encounter with a Birmingham side situated in the lower half of the table.

Four goals, two to each side, in a four minute spell between the 14th and 18th minutes, saw the game open at a frantic pace. Birmingham then went 3-2 in front nine minutes before half time, only for United to draw level within a minute of the restart.

The pace slackened somewhat as the second half progressed, but play still swung up and down the pitch. Neither side, however, could produce a winner.

DECEMBER 14TH CHELSEA H 0-1

A spirited performance by the London side earned them both points as United suffered their second home defeat in a row, both against sides from the capital.

United, and Duncan in especial, made the big mistake of trying to fight it out with the physically as strong Chelsea side, instead of trying to simply play their normal footballing game.

DECEMBER 21ST LEICESTER CITY H 4-0

New United goalkeeper, Harry Gregg, enjoyed a shut out in his debut match, having very little to do as United defeated Leicester 4-0.

The visitors major goal threat, Arthur Rowley, was well policed by Duncan in what was a sound tactical move by Matt Busby and Leicester could offer no alternative goalscoring possibilities.

United were a goal up at half time and had no difficulty in increasing their advantage during the second half.

DECEMBER 25TH LUTON TOWN H 3-0
DECEMBER 26TH LUTON TOWN A 2-2

A happy Christmas all round for United, with two points at Old Trafford and a point at Kenilworth Road the following day.

In the first of the two meetings, Luton were no match for United, who scored three without reply. One of those being a penalty from Duncan, which was despatched so powerfully that Baynham in the Luton goal failed to see it.

In the Boxing Day fixture, United looked to be heading for a repeat result, being 2-0 ahead at half time. Luton, to their credit, fought back during the second half and earned a share of the points.

DECEMBER 28TH MANCHESTER CITY A 2-2

Once again, United were in front at half time and once again they had to be content with a share of the points.

Viollet gave United the lead in the seventh minute, only to see Hayes equalise thirty seconds later. Charlton again put the visitors in front shortly afterwards and it remained at 2-1 until the sixty fourth minute, when bill Foulkes in an attempt to clear could only watch in despair as the ball slid past Harry Gregg.

City, given a lift, went out for a winner, but the United defence stood firm and both sides had to be content with a share of the points.

JANUARY 4TH WORKINGTON TOWN A 3-1 FA CUP 3RD ROUND

Played in typical cup tie fashion, Workington took the lead after only five minutes, but by the sixteenth minute of the first half, United were 3-1 in front thanks to a Dennis Viollet hat trick. The home side continued to threaten, but they could not find a way through a strong United defence and in the end had to be content in earning just praises for a commendable performance.

JANUARY 11TH LEEDS UNITED A 1-1

Neither United or Duncan Edwards enjoyed the best of afternoons, with the Yorkshire side more than happy to leave Old Trafford with a point. Meek kept the United danger man well under control and he was of little inspiration in a rather poor performance.

JANUARY 14TH RED STAR BELGRADE H 2-1 E.CUP QUART. FINAL 1ST LEG.

A closely fought cup-tie, with the Yugoslav's more than able to combine skill with brawn in an effort to

"Rugby league fans would have quarrelled at the punishment that Duncan Edwards took as he waded through"

unsettle United. One newspaper of the day reported - "Rugby league fans would have quarrelled at the punishment that Duncan Edwards took as he waded through."

Time and again, Duncan forced his way through the packed defence of Red Star and on one occasion, he beat three men before passing to Scanlon on the wing. The resulting cross provided the opportunity for Charlton to score.

JANUARY 18TH BOLTON WANDERERS H 7-2

Bolton arrived at Old Trafford confident that they could achieve the double over United for a second consecutive season, but it did not take long for them to realise that it was not going to be.

United took an early lead, but a slip up by Duncan in the 20th minute lead to Bolton's equaliser. Spending too long on the ball in midfield, he was robbed by Dennis Stevens, whose pass upfield saw Bolton draw level.

As the game progressed, Bolton were run ragged. Charlton completed his first hat trick for the club, while a Viollet double and one from Scanlon gave United an unassailable lead despite Bolton scoring a second. Duncan almost added to this, but his inswinging shot from the corner flag, was gathered underneath the Bolton crossbar by Hopkinson.

With four minutes left to play, however, he did manage to get his name on the score sheet. Scanlon was brought down in the penalty area by Higgins and the resulting kick left the unfortunate Hopkinson with little chance.

JANUARY 25TH IPSWICH TOWN H 2-0 FA CUP 4TH ROUND

United had to work hard for their place in the fifth round, as Ipswich put up a gallant fight, only to be beaten by two Bobby Charlton goals, one in each half.

Duncan was overshadowed by his wing half team mate Eddie Colman, but when the latter tired in the second half, the strong legs of the England man kept United on their cup course.

FEBRUARY 1ST ARSENAL A 5-4

Debatably, one the best games ever played in the First Division, with both sides committed to attack throughout the ninety minutes. Surprisingly, the headline in the following day's Sunday Pictorial read - "United Take It Easy And Edwards Is The Worst Offender".

Their correspondent, Jack Peart wrote, "If I were Matt Busby, I'd have a few harsh words to say to certain Manchester United players who give every impression of becoming far too cocky and casual.

"Biggest offender is left half Duncan Edwards. I cannot think his display in this thrilling game would impress England team manager Walter Winterbottom who was watching. He was clearly at fault for Arsenal's fourth goal, when instead of clearing, he dallied on the ball and that cost United another goal they should not have conceded."

The match itself was a pulsating affair, with United leading 3-0 by half time. Duncan opened the scoring with a low shot past Kelsey from around 25 yards out and further goals from Taylor and Charlton saw United storm ahead. Duncan could have considered himself unlucky not to have added a further couple of goals with two good attempts.

After the interval, Arsenal came back into it, scoring thrice in the same number of minutes to the obvious thrill of their supporters and shock to United. To their credit, United stood firm and rallied together, forcing the home side back onto the defensive and once again pulling ahead through Viollet and Taylor.

Not to be out done, Arsenal continued to press forward and managed to reduce the scoreline to 5-4. Their valiant attempts of securing an equaliser were to be in vain as United held on to their lead. Both sides left the field to a standing ovation, following a game which would be etched in the memory of all those present for the rest of their lives. It was a game which would also find its way into the history books, a fact unknown as the fans flocked out of Highbury marvelling at the exhibition of football that they had just witnessed.

FEBRUARY 5TH RED STAR BELGRADE A 3-3 E. CUP QUAR. FINAL 2ND LEG

In the opening half, Red Star were outplayed with some brilliant football. Dennis Viollet increased United's aggregate lead in the second minute to 3-1 and a further two from Bobby Charlton made it 5-1 on aggregate by the half hour mark.
After the re-start, Red Star, with nothing to lose took the game to United and pulled a goal back within two minutes. A penalty, given away by Bill Foulkes, reduced the arrears further and when Harry Gregg handled outside the penalty area the resulting free kick put Red Star level on the day at 3-3.

United were now on the defensive and fighting hard to hold onto their solitary aggregate goal advantage, which they managed to do, earning a place in the semi-finals for the second consecutive year.

The celebrations eventually began to lose momentum as tiredness took over, with a few hours sleep caught before the morning flight back to Manchester. The flight plan was Belgrade to Munich, a re-fuelling stop and then on to Manchester, with arrival scheduled for late afternoon.
Germany was, however, as far as the BEA Elizabethan airliner got, with the events of the afternoon of February 6th now as much a part of the history of Manchester United as any on field triumph.
The dream was dead!
While many of his team mates died instantly, Duncan, although seriously hurt, some how survived.
Of all the injured, Duncan, along with Matt Busby were the most serious, with his condition giving cause for concern.
In the days that followed, the news bulletins from the Rechts der Isar hospital were frequent and eagerly awaited by United and football supporters alike back in Britain. Having already lost the likes of Byrne, Taylor, Colman, Jones, Pegg and Bent, prayers were said for the survival of Duncan. Each day brought both hope and despair as the following diary of events tell.

FEBRUARY 7TH "EDWARDS CRITICAL"

"Duncan Edwards is still seriously ill, but somewhat improved. Injuries include - broken ribs, fracture of right leg and bad chest injuries. He is also suffering from shock. Doctors, however, were doubtful whether he would play football again. They also added that they would not have to consider amputation, in the case of the leg injury."

POST ✦ OFFICE
TELEGRAM

Charges to pay
s.   d.

RECEIVED

No.
OFFICE STAMP

Prefix.   Time handed in.   Office of Origin and Service Instructions.   Words.

At.
To
By

AG

A.
From
By

♯ E149 4.7 MANCHESTER T 11

DORMAN 19 GORSE AVE STRETFORD=

ALL FLIGHTS CANCELLED FLYING TOMORROW=DUNCAN+

C1   19 NFM DUNCAN+ ♯   XR 0   B or C
                                                                 C

For free repetition of doubtful words telephone "TELEGRAMS ENQUIRY" or call, with this form
at office of delivery. Other enquiries should be accompanied by this form, and, if possible, the envelope.

FEBRUARY 8TH

He could not be considered to be out of danger, but was still reported to be better.

FEBRUARY 9TH

There continued to be no change in his overall condition and was still considered to be seriously ill.

FEBRUARY 10TH

A good deal better and was reported to have come out of a coma and had recognised and spoken to people. He had also taken some soup.

FEBRUARY 11TH "EDWARDS WORSE"

"Twenty one year old Duncan Edwards was unconscious in Munich hospital today. He has taken a sudden turn for the worst.

"Early today, doctors at the Isar hospital reported his condition as unchanged. But this afternoon doctors were alarmed at the unusually high percentage of nitrogen in the player's blood. Edwards has six times more nitrogen in his blood than is normal in a human.

"Besides the high percentage of nitrogen in his blood, Edwards has a series of broken ribs on his right side and a complicated fracture of his right thigh. Three specialists are attending him in the hospital's emergency ward."

FEBRUARY 12TH "EDWARDS FIGHTS FOR LIFE. DASH BY PARENTS"

"Manchester United international left half Duncan Edwards is fighting for his life.

"An artificial kidney was rushed 210 miles from Freiburg to Munich today - a last minute bid to save him.

"The apparatus was connected with Edwards's blood stream through an arm and a leg.

"It is understood a team of leading surgeons battling for Edwards' life made three unsuccessful attempts to detour his blood through the machine. After a number of adjustments, the blood started circulating.

"Duncan Edwards's parents and a family friend, Mr I.P. Woodley are making a dramatic dash to his bedside. Early this afternoon they left Dudley on a three hour race against time by road for London Airport, hoping to catch the 5.15pm Viscount to Munich. Police along the route were alerted by BEA and asked to facilitate the passengers of the car.

"Doctors early today said Edwards was "in very acute danger and getting worse." But they added "He is still young and therefore has more chances."

"And this afternoon they said "Edwards looks unchanged at the moment".

"As soon as the kidney arrived, it was put in a lift and taken to the fourth floor for immediate connection to Edwards. The kidney is the doctor's last chance to save Edwards, who was critically injured last week.

"Dr Georg Lang said the machine would be left running with Edwards blood circulating through it for about six hours. Then the blood would be allowed to return to the normal circulating system. The purpose of the apparatus was to take the strain off Edwards's injured kidneys.

"The artificial kidney was called for when Dr Georg Maurer found a further deterioration in Edwards's condition which has been critical from the start. The United and England half back was said to be near to death this morning after the nitrogen content of his blood rose to 500 promile during the night. Doctor's said a "45 promile content is normal".

FEBRUARY 13TH "EDWARDS NOW MUCH BETTER".

"Duncan Edwards woke up from a week of unconsciousness today and asked "Where am I?" He also asked for a cup of tea.

"Prof. Maurer said his condition was "very gratifying" and had fed the player a little milk.

FEBRUARY 14TH "DUNCAN EDWARDS HAS SERIOUS RELAPSE"

"The condition of Duncan Edwards deteriorated seriously today said doctors at the Isar Hospital in Munich.

"He suffered increasing periods of unconsciousness. The main problem is the nitrogen content of his blood, which had been reduced on Wednesday by use of the artificial kidney, rose again to about four times normal."

FEBRUARY 15TH "EDWARDS : SOS GOES OUT FOR BLOOD"

Police radio cars raced to the homes of Munich blood donors early today when Manchester United star Duncan Edwards began to have severe haemorrhages.

"Prof. Maurer explained later that the use of the artificial kidney had reduced the ability of Edwards's blood to clot. Shortly after midnight Edwards began to bleed internally.

"Prof. Maurer was awakened at 2 am. Donors were reached through police radio patrol cars and taken to the hospital. After several transfusions, Edwards bleeding was brought to a halt.

"Dr Graham Taylor of BEA saw Edwards today. Afterwards he said Edwards's condition was unchanged and he remained dangerously ill.

"It was too early to say whether the artificial kidney, which was used for seven hours yesterday, would have to be used again.

"Dr Taylor said that surgeons and doctors of the hospital had commented that Edwards had a strong will to live.

"They really admire his fighting spirit a lot. He has plenty of pluck that boy, apart from his splendid former physical condition and the doctors feel these are helping to pull him through.

"Dr Taylor said that Edwards was conscious all the time, but was very restless. He added, "I told him this morning to keep quiet and not to talk more than necessary. He said that he understood".

FEBRUARY 16TH "FIGHTER EDWARDS AMAZES DOCTORS"

"Duncan Edwards, who is still seriously ill here in Munich, is amazing doctors in his fight for life.

"He has regained consciousness. His breathing is stronger and better and the magnificent fitness he maintained before the United air disaster is helping to boost his will to live.

FEBRUARY 17TH "GOOD NEWS ABOUT EDWARDS, BUT....."

"There was good news from Munich today about Duncan Edwards. Surgeons say there are signs that his badly bruised kidney may be starting to work again. As a result, it was decided not to bring the artificial kidney back into operation just yet.

"Doctors warned, however, that the improvement is only slight and it would be wrong to be too optimistic."

FEBRUARY 18TH "DUNCAN EDWARDS : A RESTFUL NIGHT"

"Duncan Edwards spent a restful night, the Munich hospital reported today.

"Edwards was put on artificial kidney treatment for the third time yesterday, the doctors said."

FEBRUARY 19TH "EDWARDS WORSE : IN DISTRESS"

"Doctors gave grim news about the condition of Duncan Edwards. He has taken a turn for the worse and is "showing signs of distress."

"The bulletin said he was weaker, following further treatment with the artificial kidney. He has been given direct person to person blood transfusions. Use of the artificial kidney has developed into a vicious circle, which is gradually sapping his strength.

"A BEA doctor said "Edwards's condition was about the worst it had been since the kidney treatment was started last week."

"Though there be many members, yet is there one body."

Manchester United Football Club, England — and — 1953–1958.

FEBRUARY 20TH "VERY SLIGHT IMPROVEMENT"

"A BEA doctor said last night that there was a very slight improvement in his condition."

FEBRUARY 21ST

DAILY EXPRESS - "3am: After Fight For Life That Amazed Doctors, Duncan Edwards, England's Giant Dies In Hospital."

DAILY MIRROR - "EDWARDS OF UNITED DIES"

DAILY HERALD - "4am DUNCAN EDWARDS IS DEAD"

MANCHESTER EVENING NEWS - "TEAM MATES WEEP AS EDWARDS DIES"

Team mates of Manchester United's plucky young footballer Duncan Edwards wept in the Rechts der Isar hospital here today when they were told that 'soccer's wonder boy' had lost his fifteen day fight for life.
"The lion hearted Edwards died peacefully in sleep, with no pain, at 2.15am after a desperate last-minute battle to save him.
"About midnight, doctors noticed that his circulation was failing. Injections caused a temporary improvement, but his strength ebbed away.
"Nurses at his bed side - well used to suffering and sudden death - broke down and wept as the flame for life for which they had fought so hard flickered out.
"His parents and his fiancée were told of his death at their hotel."

FEBRUARY 22ND

In Manchester, a sullen crowd of 66,124 packed the terraces and stands of Old Trafford, with United due to face Nottingham Forest in what was the second fixture after the disaster.
Prior to the kick off, the Dean of Manchester conducted an inter-denominational service on the pitch, as a tribute to all who had died. The occasion was obviously sad and solemn, but had been made even more so by Duncan's death.
At the same time as many tear stained faces were remembering their heroes, hundreds of miles away the Duncan's body was carried onto an aeroplane at Munich's airport for a flight to London, before being taken by road to Dudley in preparation for the funeral four days later.

FEBRUARY 26TH

The streets of Dudley were lined with thousands of people all wishing to pay their last respects to the local hero. They watched in silence as his body was taken from his parents home to St Francis's Church on the Priory Estate, through the streets where he had frequently kick a ball in his childhood.

His coffin should have been borne into the church by four of his international colleagues and two United

...“Go forward Duncan Edwards, from this place rich in achievement, honoured and loved by us all”

team mates, but snow delayed the latter, whose places were taken by two Aston Villa players.

The Rev. A. Dawson Catterall conducted the service, concluding his sermon with a fitting epilogue - “This superb and modest athlete lived and loved his life among us to the full and would have undone no part of it. And it is now fulfilled. Go forward Duncan Edwards, from this place rich in achievement, honoured and loved by us all.”

Between 250 and 300 wreaths made a carpet of colour around the grave in Queens Cross Cemetery, where an estimated 3,000 were gathered awaiting the cortege as it made its way through the Black Country town.

At the graveside the grief of the many mourners was the only noise as they bid a final farewell to their hero.

The Rev. A. Dawson Catterall, in his sermon, summed up everyone's thoughts of Duncan superbly when he said, “We are proud that the great Duncan Edwards was one of our sons. He goes to join the mortal company of Steve Bloomer and Alex James. Talent and even genius we shall see again, but there will be only one Duncan Edwards.”

Since that Wednesday in Dudley, the name of Duncan Edwards has lived on in the memory of all who knew him and saw him play. His exploits in the red of Manchester United and the white of England have been recalled time and time again. They have also been narrated to thousands of others who were unfortunate never to have witnessed the legend in the flesh.

Duncan Edwards is a name synonymous with that of Manchester United and since that fateful afternoon, some forty odd years ago now, countless players have etched their names into the history of the club and as the years continue to pass by, countless more will add their names to the list. There will be debates about the capabilities, of who was the best in a certain position, but at the end of the day when the question is asked - “Who was United's greatest ever player?”, there will only ever be one answer - Duncan Edwards, the boy who had the lot.